Kristen's Rites of Passage

The Curriculum Ceremony of Productivity

FOREWORD BY ROSE MALONE-JONES, APRN

By

LeGarrius T. Jones

1

Kristen's Rites of Passage

The Curriculum Ceremony of Productivity

King Industries
Community Development Center
www.Kingicdc.com

Kristen's Rites of Passage, the Curriculum Ceremony of Productivity
By: LeGarrius T. Jones
ISBN: 978-0-615-30842-5

Printed in the United States of America.
Editor and Proofreader: Mrs. Jane Greiner, Phd.

Jonestown Publishing books may be ordered through booksellers or by contacting:
Jonestown Publishing
P.O. Box 751821
Centerville,Oh. 45459
www.kingicdc.com
www.jonestownpublishing.com

Dedication

First, I dedicate this book to my two daughters, Breon and Kristen; they are my inspiration and my life. Everything I do I do for them. They are the reason why I live the way that I do. I also dedicate this book to my entire Jonestown family and to the future generations of the Jonestown family. I am a firm believer in nurturing the growth and development of our kids then passing that information down to the next generations so that they too will benefit from the opportunities created now by their ancestors to also see the growth and benefit from it.

Next, I want to encourage all small business owners to try your best and believe. I want to dedicate this book to entrepreneurs who endures the struggle of owning your own business and succeeding. I want to acknowledge President Barack Obama for signing the Executive Order establishing the Economic Recovery Advisory Board. The Economic Recovery Advisory Board will discuss matters such as the revitalizing the public education system and strategic ways to assist entrepreneurs and small business owners through the provision of effective grants.

Further, I want to dedicate this book to all hard working entrepreneurs. Hard work is the backbone of all success. Without that all is lost. We want to inspire hope, opportunity, and change in our kids of today for tomorrow. Through business we can strengthen our own communities. With more self-sufficient communities through solar and/or wind turbines we can start to change the way the United States spends money on energy. By teaching our kids life survival skills through business, we will start to raise a nation of young business owners making a living in today's society. We can then begin putting back some of the money usurped from the community by non-residential business owners.

Finally, I dedicate this book to humanity; to all people that have became somebody through hard work. I dedicate this book to you--the believer, the courageous, and the fearless; to those not afraid to learn, grow, and develop themselves continually, to the ones not afraid to step out there on faith and live life to the fullest. I dedicate this book to us all.

Contents

Acknowledgements

First, I want to start by thanking God for giving me the vision and inspiration to want a better life and become more. I thank God for allowing me to share that dream with my family. God's word has kept me and allowed me to conquer my fears. I am now a person willing and ready to serve the Lord and do His will.

I want to thank my family and friends for their support during the production of this book. All who have motivated me through the years to continue my journey of starting our family businesses so that we may profit from, I want to thank you!

I want to thank my pastor Bishop Paul S. Morton for continuing to give words of wisdom to my family and the people of New Orleans during the trying times of Hurricane Katrina.

Katrina has hurt many families. I want to acknowledge my mom for helping so many people while she was on duty. She assisted with moving bed-ridden patients up to the roof to be flown out of rising waters. She unfortunately hurt her back and had to have two surgeries as a result. We lived on 7518 Malvern Dr. in New Orleans La. and my mom had several businesses throughout the New Orleans east area. After she hurt her back in hurricane Katrina she has relocated to Ohio for a clean start. She has opened her first business since her back surgeries. She is now doing very well in Ohio with her new business.

I want to say congratulations to you, John….it's not every day your next door neighbor becomes famous. Congratulations, on your success! For Will Smith to play John Keller, Your Life's Story, that's Top Notch! They nick named you, "The Can Man", huh bra.

So, let me see if I got this right, an ex-marine devises the rescue of 244 people of New Orleans from a building in which you lived, the American Can Company, from severe flooding during Hurricane Katrina. When you called and asked me to check it out online, I saw Will Smith, James Lassiter, and Ken Stovitz announcing the production of your film. I guess that finalized it, right! Once again, congratulations on your success!

At last, I want to thank King Industries, Community Development Center's staff and volunteers for a job well done. Many hours we worked hard on the completion of this project. You are very much appreciated! Thank You….

Foreword

This book was written by my son and my granddaughter. It's the recorded events of their Book of Information given by King Industries, Community Development Center. Our Book of Information was created so that kids could start to study technology and business. It's a three part program in which meditation, prayer, and study time is done daily for forty days during the program.

I do believe that meditating on God's word helps, people to remain focused on their goals. In the Rites of Passage Program, my granddaughter had a set of goals she had to have accomplished before she could complete the program. Her goals were to write about what she has learned in the program and to start a publishing company.

It says in Joshua 1:8

"Do not let this Book of the Law depart from your mouth; meditate on it day and night, so that you may be careful to do everything written in it. Then you will be prosperous and successful."

It is said that through the lack of knowledge our people shall perish. This book gives practical knowledge for anyone serious about accomplishing their goals and dreams. It gives you a daily meditation and prayer, as well as a daily one hour study session. It leads you to study people that have had many obstacles to overcome before accomplishing their goals. How did they do it? They stayed focused and continued their application daily!

As we look forward to the future, we must create ourselves now as to who we will become in the future. We must work hard and pass our work down to the next generation so they may have a brighter future as well. We must teach them to create their own opportunities through business and not to be afraid to go after their dreams. We must encourage them and be their best supporters.

We work hard to instill in our kids a good working knowledge of the word of God. We should also work hard to instill a good working knowledge of wealth creation within our kids and throughout our communities. To end the generational bondage of poverty within our community we must teach kids to rebuild, reorganize, and economically strength the community by learning to generate wealth. We have to strategically train our kids to make money within any environment through business regardless of where they are. My passions, my hopes, and my dreams, I pass down in prayer that my generation will be productive human beings in society. To end this vicious cycle of poverty among people of the United States we must devise our own wealth creation strategies to pass down so our kids can benefit from them in the future.

Rose Malone-Jones, APRN
Nurse Practitioner/Family Counselor

Introduction

This book is about an eleven year old girl named Kristen who goes through a forty day Rites of Passage Program which teaches her to start a business, produce a product for that business, and invest the money made in abandoned real estate properties within the community. Her goal at the beginning of forty days was to start a business. We named our new business Jonestown Publishing, LLC. Through it, she has learned to start a publishing company, co-authored a book, and created a product to sell online which will generate wealth to buy the real estate properties for her and our non-profit organization.

At the beginning of her forty day passage I was there with her in Porterville California where we lived as a family. Unfortunately the mother and I separated before Kristen was able to finish the program. I decided to continue with my plans and publish the program so that I can send her a copy of it in book form. I wanted her to see that problem will arise and that you can't let anything stop you from accomplishing your goals.

Our non-profit organization's name is King Industries Community Development Center. We wanted to teach Kristen about what a non-profit organization does, why we chose to start a non-profit, and how it operates. Our organization has created several programs for the inner city youth to take advantage of while being employed and learning a trade as well. We will share in the Green Revolution; we believe that every house within the inner city should be remodeled as self-sufficient homes employing workers of that community.

The purpose of King Industries is to train community members to start businesses, produce products, and use monies earned to reinvest it back into the community, buying and rebuilding the community. Information is valuable and we want to pass this information of economic growth down to our kids in the form of books. We want to preserve it so the younger generation may benefit from what we have learned.

Imagine, if you will, the impact on the community if more of our youth mastered this skill at their age. What would that do for the community in the next couple of generations? You would see more and more kids with jobs working on their own houses and owning their own businesses. This is the purpose of King Industries and Kristen was the first person through the Rites of Passage Program.

My great grandmother, I think started our generation off with the ideas of business. Lo and behold, and generations later, we are a strong business oriented family. We must work hard to pass these skills down to the next generation for economic survival. We must teach our kids about money and its uses, businesses, and economic growth.

Today, we start the next generation of business owners with a Rites of Passage Program. This program is important to us because it will educate young people in the process of making money by creating products, starting businesses, and reinvest that money earned back into abandoned properties throughout the city. My job as a member of King Industries is to paint a clear picture of the journey one must travel to start a successful business, create products for those businesses (so that there is something to sell to raise capital for the business), and reinvest that money into buying abandoned homes in the community and fixing them up.

Twenty percent of all proceeds from the sales of our books will go back to King Industries, our family's non-profit organization, for continued community development efforts. These were her goals to accomplish within forty days. This is King Industry's Curriculum Ceremony of Productivity.

Our curriculum consists of a morning meditation and daily word. For Kristen her goal was to start a business and learn to create a product for that business. For an hour in the evening we would have book study, were we study a person of choice given by the program coordinator, and we would study product creation within that hour as well. We would then record the date and time, our thoughts, and feelings on what was taught and shared.

Our goal is to cultivate a community of powerful extraordinary thinkers, by teaching our youth to become self-educating leaders. King Industries is a Community Development Center that teaches, "Kids in Need of Guidance" (KING), to start businesses, buy real estate properties, and renovate their property to rent out for a capital gain. This way kids in the community can learn the cycle of buying and selling properties, through the money generated through the products they create.

How This Book Was Written:

Daily Meditation:
We organized this book first with a daily meditation and a daily word. First thing, early in the morning from 6:00-6:10am we would pray, go into *"Our World of Prayer."* In the Meditation and prayer (OWP) section of the program we would sit Indian style or whatever makes you comfortable, and would meditate to the sound of creation, the seventh principle in Dr. Dyer's book "Manifesting your Destiny".

Morning and Evening (6:00-6:10am) and (4:30-4:40pm)
The Bible verses were selected by our program director. We would meditate to remain focused and balanced throughout our day.

Daily Word: Morning and Evening (6:00-6:10am) and (4:30-4:40pm)
The daily word is in addition to our daily meditation (prayer). I wanted to give them extra motivation to remember throughout their day. So we would use it in the morning and evenings. I want to keep them focused for the task at hand. Keep their minds on what it is they are trying to achieve, never forgetting that they have to stay focused on their dreams in order to succeed. We use it daily to embed it deep within the subconscious mind as if it were a ritual.

Refresh Yourself Daily:
We want to incorporate into our daily lives an affirmative daily message full of positively charged words. In order to be happy, we must program ourselves for happiness. In order to be successful, we must program ourselves for success. We must believe we can be happy and successful. This is what we meditate on daily. We want to bring these thoughts into existence and every day we need to meditate on these words to bring them into focus. And we must believe that we deserve to be happy and successful.

Daily Quote: We learn of the quotes of each person we study for forty days.

Definition Section: We give for each day a new definition word that relates to our Bible verse and the person of study.

Book Study: 5:00pm – 5:30pm
We research for thirty minutes the person of study and define the word for the day. Also, if there are words that we come across in our study and we don't know the meaning of them, we define those as well.

Product Creation: 5:30pm – 6:00pm
In this section we also research how to create products for future sales in our publishing company. We do the research on product creation and self-publishing after we have studied the people of choice for thirty minutes. Then we study product creation and how to self-publish for thirty minutes each day of the forty days.

Kristen's Thoughts of the Day:
Kristen tells what she thought about the book study for that hour. She comments on the daily subject do her best to write about whatever she feels. The key is to get her writing and organizing her thoughts. I would be happy with and accept anything on what we spoke about for that day.

Daddy's Thoughts of the Day:
This is the last entry of the day. I give my thoughts continuing to re-enforce the idea of business growth and sharing basic laws and principles we incorporate into our business. Here I will comment on each day. I want to give her more encouragement on accomplishing her goals and completing the Rites of Passage Program. In this section I want to reinforce the thought of positive thinking, Kwanzaa principles, and Universal Laws as well. All registrants of King Industries will have the opportunity to record a written record of that experience, giving them a marketable product enabling them to sell their products online. This is done and created as a journal to pass down to their families and future generations.

We use meditation principles to get the word deep inside our soul and we would meditate continuously. Meditating on God's word is the other principle that we will take full advantage of through the forty days of the Rites of Passage Program and for the rest of our lives. These are our family principles.

The principle of hard-work we will use to create this product and use as an example in our marketing strategy to show how to duplicate the process of product creation and marketing strategies, to make a huge amount of money online. Our goal is to start a publishing company and sell our newly created product online.

Day 1:
The First Day of Research
Wednesday April 9, 2008

Daily Meditation: Morning and Evening (6:00-6:10am) and (4:30-4:40pm)
Philippians 4:13
"I can do everything through him who gives me strength."

Daily Word:

WONDERFUL WEDNESDAY

Throughout our day, we want to reflect on how blessed we are and how beautiful life is. We want to do our best to honor ourselves and our spirit. We want to remain humble throughout the day, never forgetting that God is not mocked. We want to remember to work hard at accomplishing our goals and increase our talents and skills, stay focused on the task at hand so that we may excel in all that we do. Put forth effort at being the best person we can be, knowing that we are whole, together, generous, balanced, and well-rounded. We will not be afraid to let our light shine through and make a difference in the lives of others. Regardless of what the day may bring, we will remain in the position of Godliness.

Evening Meditation

In this section of the program, we have book study for thirty minutes. The program coordinator selects a person to study, as well as a definition word. For our book study, we will start off with Jesus as our person of study and Sacrifice as our definition word. We will study the person of choice and then spend thirty minutes on product creation and self publishing.

5:00 – 6:00
Book Study:
Jesus

Definition: Sacrifice
1: an act of offering to a deity something precious; especially: the killing of a victim on an altar 2. Something offered in sacrifice 3 a: destruction or surrender of something for the sake of something else b: something given up or lost 4: loss 5: sacrifice hit

6:30 – 7:00pm

Writing Section: In this section we will study and learn about Jesus for thirty minutes, define the words we don't know or understand, and study product creation.

Jesus of Nazareth (7–2 BC/BCE to 26–36 AD/CE), was the sacrificial Lamb of God. He sacrificed himself for the sins of mankind. The gospels are the main source of information regarding Jesus and his teachings. In the field of history and biblical studies, most scholars believe and agree that Jesus was a Galilean Jew.

The gospels are the main teachings on the knowledge concerning Jesus' life. With regard to Jesus being a Galilean Jew, scholars in the field of biblical studies and history believe that he was also a teacher and a healer. It is also believed that John the Baptist baptized Jesus, and the Roman Governor Pontius Pilate crucified Jesus in Jerusalem under charges of sedition against the Roman Empire.

Jesus' coming was prophesied in the Old Testament as the Messiah. Christians view Jesus as divine. Christians believe that Jesus was crucified and on the third day he rose, resurrected from the dead.

Predominantly, Christians believe Jesus to be the "Son of God" (meaning that God, the Son, is second in the Trinity), providing salvation and reconciliation through God. Other Christian beliefs include Jesus' miracles, his virgin birth, his ascension into Heaven, and his Second Coming. While Christians accept the doctrine of the Trinity, a small minority of nontrinitarian believers question the divinity of Jesus.

We would now look up the word nontrinitarian: NON meaning not. Then, we would look up the word trinity: the Father, the Son (incarnate as Jesus Christ), and the Holy Spirit. It's a Christian doctrine stating that simultaneously and eternally God is one being. It is believed that God is a three person indwelling. Early century doctrine stated that the Trinity is "one God who exists in three Persons and one substance, Father, Son, and Holy Spirit."

After talking my daughter through the book study, an hour has passed and we are finished for the day. For our first day of the Rites of Passage Program, I think it went very well. Now I will write what we studied in the product creation section and then Kristen will share her thoughts.

Product Creation: The First Day of Research

From my research I have found that information is the most valuable asset there is. Why do I say this? If you notice, everything is in some form of information being given away or sold. Whether it's a newspaper, magazine, book, audio, or video, it's all information that is given to us through different mediums. Self-publishing your own information that millions of people need and want to buy, has always been the fastest way to wealth.

Today in the information age, valuable information is more accessible to us than ever before. By acquiring more and more information, you will start to build a library of knowledge. Knowledge only becomes valuable if you put it to use. Then, knowledge becomes power. In our pursuit of happiness, we are not so much trying to gain power, as to develop a better way of living. Power and money is not important to us, however you do need money to live. Therefore it's our belief about money that makes us use it for the good of mankind.

Think about all the government agencies that use information to bring about wealth, and all the major companies that use market research (information) to structure their products. All of the millionaires, and what information do they use to create their wealth? That's the same information we have available to us right now. We just have to know where to find it, determine what information is valuable to us, and decide what to do with the information after we receive it.

In my research, I will give you valuable information that could dramatically change your life forever in a short amount of time. I have studied wealth creation for years and have planned my steps strategically towards success. This book alone is proof that we, my daughter and I, have created a product, sold our product, and has made money with our product. We intend to share the same money making methods with you. Create your own book, product, or even Rite of Passage Program to create wealth for you, your family, and business.

I am excited to see our work, the finished product in stores and on websites being sold for a good cause. I am excited to now have reaped the benefits after so many years of hard work and planning. It is very true that whatever measure of work you put into something, you get back ten fold. I am excited to know that I don't have to work on my old job anymore and instead can build my businesses full time now. Financial independence is real to all whom acquire the knowledge of building wealth. I am here as an average man sharing my knowledge with you on how to build wealth through the creation of products.

Kristen's Thoughts of the Day:
I think that Jesus sacrificed his life because he cared for us. He cared for us because he was the incarnation of God.

Sedition: means encouraging the people to rebel against the government. Sedition is more about encouraging the people to rebel, where treason is actually betraying the country.

Daddy's Thoughts of the Day:
On our first day of book study we learned about Jesus for an hour. Going back to our Bible verse of study for this evening Philippians 4:13 "I can do everything through him who gives me strength." This has to get deep into our soul, hearts, and thoughts before it can become real to us and work in our lives. We meditated on these words twice for ten minutes each time.

Our defined word for the day was sacrifice and she has learned the meaning so now, hopefully, she can start to learn how to apply it in her life at the appropriate times throughout her living. We as parents in our family try to be patient with our kids and give them the essential tools needed to battle life and our worldly flesh. Flesh in life is her enemy and equipping Kirsten with the Word prepares her to behave responsibly and to make positive choices in her life. We try to show her that victory and salvation is all in His Word.

As we read, we learned that Jesus was a Galilean Jew. He was also a teacher and a healer, baptized by John the Baptist, and was crucified in Jerusalem on by the Roman Governor Pontius Pilate, on the charge of sedition. Then we looked up the word sedition because, to be honest, I didn't know what it meant either. So I asked her what does sedition mean and she said" What, I don't know, what does it mean? And she said it like ha... ha... ha... I can't wait to see your response. We just had one of those "Are You Smarter than a Fifth Grader" moments.

I want to thank you, Kristen, for doing a good job on your chores and your first day of the book study. You are a hard worker and a beautiful little girl with an incredible heart. I can remember as I sailed across the oceans, in my former job, I would go out on the deck of the ship and look out across the water and think of my family. One time I was out thinking and praying after about five minutes, I saw a shooting star dart across the dark sky. It was amazing that it happened just as I had finishing sending up praises; I opened my eyes to the surprise of a shooting star. It shot across the sky like a rocket. The moon shining over the sea is the image I will have stuck in the time of my mind, forever. One of the most beautiful moments was captured in time. In the "*Moon Shining Over the Sea*", I saw my vision.

Day 2:
Self Evaluation
Thursday April 10, 2008

Daily Meditation: Morning and Evening (6:00-6:10am) and (4:30-4:40pm)
Ephesians 6:10
"Finally, be strong in the Lord and in his mighty power."

THANKFUL THURSDAY

Today we want to give thanks, remembering all the things we should be thankful for. We should choose to be thankful for our experiences, good or bad, our friends, family, and most importantly our health. We should be thankful for who we are now and what we are to become. Our words of thanksgiving will be received through our prayers, our spirit, our actions and our songs. We will be still in our spirit, anxious for nothing, but thankful for all.

I am ready to act, if I can find brave men to help me.
--Carter G. Woodson

Definition Word: Goals
2: the end towards which effort is directed to accomplish a noble cause: the aim

5:00 – 6:00
Book Study:

Gordon Parks

6:30 – 7:00pm
Writing Section: In this section we will study and learn about Gordon Parks for thirty minutes, define the words we don't know or understand, and study product creation.

Gordon Roger Alexander Buchannan Parks (November 30, 1912 – March 7, 2006) was a ground breaking American photographer, musician, poet, novelist, journalist, activist and film director. He is best remembered for his photo essays for Life Magazine and as the director of the 1971 film, 'Shaft.'

Parks was the youngest of 15 kids, and of course, since he was in a black family in 1912, he was poor in the segregated environment of Fort Scott, Kansas. His mother was a Methodist. His mother refused to allow him to justify failure because he was black. Being black was not an excuse in her book. She instilled in her kids self-confidence, ambition and a strong will for hard work.

Parks later commented on her by saying, "I had a mother who would not allow me to complain about not accomplishing something because I was black. Her attitude was, 'If a white boy can do it, then you can do it, too—and do it better, or don't come home.' His mother died when he was 15 years old, according to his book "A Hungry Heart."

Ephesians 6:10
"Finally, my brethren, be strong in the Lord, and in the power of his might."

We then talked about this Bible verse and how it relates to him and others in their life. I asked Kristen if she believes the words of the Bible and she said yes. So I said, "What is God's might?" Her response was, He has the power to do all things. So if you work hard and believe in His word you will have the power to do all things?" "Yes!"

"Goal" was our definition word we chose for today and we defined it as: the end towards which effort is directed to accomplish a noble cause: the aim. I then asked what are some of her other goals besides the one we just chose for her? She responded "I don't know". So I gave her a Self-discovery Goal Setting Exercise.

We concentrated on these reflective questions designed to help her look at the big picture. Within this goal setting exercise are techniques that allow you to gain a better understanding who you are and what you want out of life.

1. What do you like about yourself?
2. What do you like to do?
3. What do you like to read?
4. What is your interest?
5. What do you think you might like but haven't done enough research to know for sure?
6. What can you spend hours doing?
7. If you didn't have to work, what would you do with your days?
8. What would you do with a million dollars?
9. What activities interest you?
10. What can catch your attention for hours?
11. What can you dedicate more time to learning?

12. If you thought failure wasn't an option, how big could you dream?
13. If you had three wishes, what would they be?
14. Go back in time for a year; what would be the most important thing you did?

Product Creation: Self Evaluation

The first thing you should do when creating a product is to evaluate yourself. You must believe that you are worthy and that you can create whatever it is you choose. Then look at yourself and know what it is you like to do, what are your talents and skills? Who will buy your product?

For instance, I believe in the Christian faith and I think I have as much right as anyone else to create a product and sell it as a book online or through retail book stores. I am talented and skillful at creating. I like to create things from nothing, using only my imagination. I know I want to create a product that can involve my children and our Christian faith. I also like business, so King Industries Community Development Center was created as a nonprofit organization used to promote our products. Therefore, we can sell our products to other believers of the Christian faith who would like to generate wealth in their lives to further their Christian cause.

I don't believe God intended his people to be poor; therefore we as Christians should obtain wealth so that we can have a bigger role in doing the will of God. Imagine if you were a millionaire. Would you have a problem fixing, or helping to rebuild a city destroyed by Hurricane Katrina? New Orleans is my hometown and when I went back, it hurt me to my heart to see the devastation and death that has over come my city.

I would have gathered all the wealthy people in the city and dedicated sections of the city for each millionaire to rebuild. Imagine the impact of over twenty millionaires all dedicated to doing God's work and rebuilding that city. I believe we have to depend on ourselves when it comes to money and welfare. The government will not be there for us. So, I've decided to take matters into my own hands and create my own wealth through the knowledge given to me by God and use it for His glory.

Kristen's Thoughts of the Day:
I personally think that Gordon Parks is a busy person because he was a photographer, musician, poet, novelist, journalist, activist and a film director. I wonder when he had a day off.

More specifically, a covenant, in contrast to a contract, is a one-way agreement whereby the covenanter is the only party bound by the promise. A covenant may have conditions and prerequisites that qualify the undertaking, including the actions of second or third parties, but there is no inherent agreement by such other parties to fulfill those requirements. Consequentially, the only party that can break a covenant is the covenanter.

Daddy's Thoughts of the Day:
Kristen's set forth goals, are to complete the Rites of Passage Program and start a publishing company. In the process of going through the Rites of Passage Program it enabled us to write it down creating information on her going through a life changing event recording a very important time in her history enabling her to share it with friends and family forever through her publishing company.

I had her answer these questions to give her some thoughts about who she is and to give her a glimpse into the unknown uncharted waters of her own mind. I feel more confident that Kristen will find out all that she needs to know about herself to come to understand what God want her to do in life. At an early age, I want her to become aware of the things she likes. Therefore we still need to expose her to many different things to give her an array of choices.

Day 3:
Spend Time Thinking
Friday April 11, 2008

Daily Meditation: Morning and Evening (6:00-6:10am) and (4:30-4:40pm)
John 11: 40-41
"Then Jesus said, did I not tell you that if you believed, you would see the glory of God?"

FAITHFUL FRIDAY

Its important that we awaken to all that we are meant to be through our journey in life. Our faithfulness to ourselves will allow us to be patient in life as we become more of who we are meant to be. We should be faithful to longsuffering, bearing of pain, and dealing with trials without complaint. We should be faithful in showing self-control with others, as well as ourselves. Our faith will cause us to fight against any adversity, cause us to be focused, and fearless and have faith throughout this day.

[That little man in black says] woman can't have as much rights as man because Christ wasn't a woman. Where did your Christ come from? . . . From God and a woman. Man has nothing to do with him
--Sojourner Truth

Definition Word: Initiative
1. The power or ability to begin or to follow through energetically with a plan or task; enterprise and determination.
2. A beginning or introductory step; an opening move: He took the initiative in trying to solve the problem.

5:00 – 6:00
Book Study

Sojourner Truth

6:30 – 7:00pm
Writing Section: In this section we will study and learn about Sojourner Truth for thirty minutes, define the words we don't know or understand, and study product creation.

Renaming herself in 1843, Sojourner Truth (1797-November 26, 1883), previously known as Isabella Baumfree, was an American abolitionist and woman's rights activist. In 1851, in Swartekill, New York, Truth was born into slavery. She later traveled to Ohio to deliver her famous and well known speech, "Ain't I a Woman?" in Akron, Ohio's convention center at a Women's Rights Convention.

In 1799 New York began the process to legislate the abolition of slavery. However, the emancipating process of New York slaves wasn't complete until July 4, 1827. Sojourner Truth's owner, Dumont, promised her freedom before the state emancipation a year earlier under the guide-lines that "she be very faithful and do well for him spinning wool." He later changed his mind due to a hand injury that made Truth unproductive. She was infuriated. She continued working until she felt she had done enough to satisfy her sense of obligation to him by spinning 100 pounds of wool.

Truth escaped to freedom late in the year of 1826 with her infant daughter, Sophia. She regrets having to leave her other kids. Under emancipation law her kids would not have been freed until having served as bound servants up into their twenties. Later she says: "I did not run off, for I thought that wicked, but I walked off, believing that to be right."

During this book study we contemplate on our Bible verse, and try to place ourselves in Truth's shoes. What it must have been like? I can't imagine that nor do I want to. We can't take our lives for granted just because we were born in a better time period. This Bible verse is an example of persistence and faith. She must have continued prayer everyday all day to maintain an attitude that would not allow her to give up. She only demonstrated after all she has been through, a sense of right and wrong. Would you be able to have a strong moral conscience after living the life of Sojourner Truth? We have to continue to love regardless of the situations we are forced to endure and we must believe!

John 11: 40-41
"Then Jesus said, Did I not tell you that if you believed, you would see the glory of God?"

Product Creation: Spend Time Thinking

When creating a product, time and patience should go into the creation process. Careful planning is essential in this process of product creation. You should look at this as your creation and want it to reflect you as an individual. It should reflect in your heart and in the person you are. People should be able to look at your product and see the type of person you are and what your interests are. I would recommend creating something you can talk about or something that you like to do. Reflect on yourself and consider your hobbies.

For instance, my brother Marlon is a fisherman and a hunter. He likes the great outdoors. So, he would create a product involving his outdoor activities. A good product would be information for hunters training their dogs. He could create video and write a book on how to train your dog to hunt deer, raccoon, or whatever it is you hunt, and call it, "How to Train Your Dog to Track". My brother could also write a book on fishing; that is his passion and he knows all there is to know about the sport.

So, the point is to find something you love, that you have a passion for, and start thinking of ways to create a product within that industry.

Kristen's Thoughts of the Day:

I think that Sojourner Truth showed initiative because she began with something and she continued it. I think she is a brave person as well. She changed the way people think.

Daddy's Thoughts of the Day:

Yes, she was very brave and I need you to be brave in life as well. Grow just as strong as she was, if not stronger. We are not only living for ourselves. We are living for each other. I live for you and you for me, we both shall live good, healthy, prosperous, lives. This is the doctrine for our family. Be aware that your kids and family members, through the generations, from now on will have access to read this and it will benefit them in the future just as it benefited you now. What would you share with your kids from the age you are now talking to them through time? What will you share with them? And ask yourself when faced with a difficult decision? Would Jesus do this? Yes or No?

Day 4:
Find Your Niche
Saturday April 12, 2008

Daily Meditation: Morning and Evening (6:00-6:10am) and (4:30-4:40pm)
Luke 6:38
"Give and it will be given to you. A good measure, pressed down, shaken together and running over, will be poured into your lap. For with the measure you use, it will be measured to you."

SUCCESSFUL SATURDAY

To have made it to Successful Saturday is truly a wonderful success. Throughout the week, we have walked by faith, renewed our minds and spirit, and have trusted in the all powerful universe. We have maintained a wonderful character and we are thankful for whom we are and all that we have. To remain strong and in character throughout the week is truly defined as a success.

The individual who can do something that the world wants done will, in the end, make his way regardless of his race.
--Booker T. Washington

Definition Word: Integrity
1. Firm adherence to a code of especially moral or artistic values: incorruptibility
2: an unimpaired condition: soundness   3: the quality or state of being complete or undivided: completeness

5:00 – 6:00
Book Study:

Booker T. Washington

6:30 – 7:00pm
Writing Section: In this section we will study and learn about Booker T. Washington for thirty minutes, define the words we don't know or understand, and study product creation.

Booker Taliaferro Washington (April 5, 1856 – November 14, 1915) was freed from slavery as a youngster and took full advantage of getting an education.

Washington led the African American community and quickly became an educator who would ultimately lead a black college. His success continued and he grew to become a nationally well- known figure as the spokesperson for African Americans.

In 1900, Washington created The National Negro Business League (NNBL) to motivate the "commercial, agricultural, educational, and industrial" advancement of African Americans.

Up from Slavery Published in 1901, was Washington's bestselling autobiography. His book motivated and inspired the African American community and allies to move. His book landed him in the White House as a guest of President Theodore Roosevelt, the first African-American in 1901 to be invited by the president to the White House.

He died on November 14, 1915 at the age of 59 in New York where he collapsed. He was the principal of Tuskegee and they returned his body and buried him on Tuskegee University's campus near University Chapel. Washington donated more than US$1.5 million upon his death to Tuskegee University, continuing his greatest life's work, expanding the education of the Black South.

After our study, we prepare for the writing section and go back to the Bible verse and see how that word applies to the life of Booker T. Washington. Luke 6:38 say? "For with the measure you use, it will be measured unto you." The first thing that caught my eye was that he was able to raise that amount of money in the 1900's before he died. He had to work hard and $1.5 million was his reward, so he had a million dollar effort.

Most importantly, we need to create products and/or services that the world needs and sell them for economic growth and the advancement of humanity, as well as our family. It doesn't matter if you're black or white; all that matters is what you do with your life. This is the information from Booker T. Washington in his quote:

The individual who can do something that the world wants done will, in the end, make his way regardless of his race.
--Booker T. Washington

During our Rites of Passage Program, we study ways within our family to provide humanity with services or products that are needed by the world through "Our World of Prayer", which is the Integrity of our family.
1. Firm adherence to a code of especially moral or artistic values: incorruptibility 2: an unimpaired condition: soundness   3: the quality or state of being complete or undivided: completeness

My family and friends all believe in the value of education. Most African Americans I know also share in these same values. We raise our kids with these values. We can't stop stressing "education" in our household. I also strongly encourage being self-taught, which in today's society has proven just as valuable.

Product Creation: Find Your Niche
Once you have in mind what industry you want to create your product for, now focus on finding a niche. A niche is a part or segment of a market. You will start to identify which market you want to target by crating a product based on your interest. Then we would use a marketing strategy to break into an industry with informative products to sell. Don't worry about if that industry is flooded with products already; competition is good because it indicates people are interested in buying. Carve out a section of that industry by creating a niche catering to people within that industry.

For instance, in the Christian community most people want to have financial freedom but that reality is blocked because of their psychological belief in money. I've run into some Christians that believed that in order for you to have money, you would have to do something evil to get it. A saved man is still saved regardless of whether he's rich or poor.

Psalm 35:27 KJV says:
Let them shout for joy, and be glad, that favor my righteous cause: yea, let them say continually, let the Lord be magnified, which hath pleasure in the prosperity of his servant.

Right there, God wants us to be prosperous, so that is my niche market. I would create a product within the Christian community explaining how my eleven year old daughter and I created this product through faith for the benefit of our family. And, as you know, God gets the glory and now we are able to concentrate more on doing our part within humanity. Our goal is to help heal a world of some "ol battle scares"

Kristen's Thoughts of the Day:
I think Booker T. Washington died a hero for African Americans in that time and should be a hero to all African Americans today. For a man to be so great and valuable to the black community, he died too young.

Daddy's Thoughts of the Day:
I want Kristen to learn the value of hard work. I want her to know that nothing comes easy and that she creates herself. It's up to her to become somebody that contributes to humanity in a positive way doing something she loves making her desired amount of money. It's going to take time and patience to get there but I want her to know how to create her own opportunities to get her where she needs to go.

Our code is OWP (Our World of Prayer) in which we will eventually increase our daily meditations from 10 minutes to 30 minutes. Also, you can learn the true meaning of integrity the quality or state of being complete or undivided. And I want you to have firm adherence to the code. Stand strong like the beautiful young lady you are virtuously honoring your moral or artistic values. Even the smallest light shines in the mist of darkness! Never be afraid to let your light shine.

Booker T Washington was a man of persistence. He also understood the value of hard-work. We will commit ourselves to our work during these forty days and for the rest of our lives. This is a code of conduct as to how we shall stand in our businesses, and in our lives.

Persistence is that which will determine our success or failure. Without persistence you will not amount to much. And I do understand that you need heart. You have to have a strong backbone to stand up and be yourself, no matter how crazy it may seem. Your WILL can determine your ability to success.

In my dreams of creating a successful business I studied the law of persistence. At the time I was working as a Merchant Seaman and had little time to write. I would try to write while I was on the ship, but after working twelve hour days, once I lie down the ship tends to rock me to sleep. And I was doing six to nine months out there. It doesn't matter who you are, the code of persistence will allow you to succeed while others fail

"Man is made great or little by his own will."—Johann Schiller

Day 5:
Benefits of Your Product
Sunday April 13, 2008

Daily Meditation: Morning and Evening (6:00-6:10am) and (4:30-4:40pm)
Galatians 6:7
"Do not be deceived; God is not mocked [fooled], for whatsoever a man soweth, that shall he also reap."

SOULFUL SUNDAY

We should look to overflow our spirits with something good. A good word produces a good feeling. Today, we should remain in the place of peace, filling our soul with the joy and happiness from the word. Surround yourself with people of like faith and celebrate life. Remember to enjoy life on this day. Synagogue, temple, mosque, or church, whatever your faith we should be humane to one another. Seek to fill yourself with an empowering word that will keep you motivated and inspired with the love you see all around us.

I'm black, I don't feel burdened by it and I don't think it's a huge responsibility. It's part of who I am. It does not define me.
--Oprah Winfrey

Evening Meditation

Definition Word: Discipline
1: punishment 2.obsolete: instruction 3: a field of study 4: training that corrects, molds, or perfects the mental faculties or moral character 5 a: control gained by enforcing obedience or order b: orderly or prescribed conduct or pattern of behavior c: self-control

5:00 – 6:00
Book Study:

Oprah Winfrey

6:30 – 7:00pm
Writing Section: In this section we will study and learn about Oprah Winfrey for thirty minutes, define the words we don't know or understand, and study product creation.

Referred to as simply Oprah, Winfrey is an American television host, philanthropist and media mogul. Oprah Gail Winfrey (born January 29, 1954) has earned numerous Emmy Awards for her internationally-syndicated talk show, The Oprah Winfrey Show, the highest-rated talk show in the history of television. She is also a powerful book author, columnist, a magazine publisher, and an Academy Award-nominated actress. According to some, she is also the most powerful woman in the world. She is the most philanthropic African American of all time, the only black billionaire for three consecutive years, being ranked the richest African American of the 20th century.

She was born to a poor and unwed teenage mother in rural Mississippi, later being raised in an inner city Milwaukee neighborhood. Oprah was raped twice at age nine and fourteen. She had a son who died in its early stage of life. She was sent to live with a man thought to be her father in Tennessee, where he worked as a barber. While still in high school, she acquired a job in radio and at the age of 19 she began co-anchoring the local evening news. She was transferred to the daytime talk show arena due to her hard work and emotional ad-lib delivery. Winfrey advanced from a third-rated Chicago talk show, to first place. She then became internationally syndicated after launching her own production company.

Oprah created and brought a more heartfelt confessional structure to media communication. The tabloid talk show genre pioneered by Phil Donahue is considered to have been popularized and revolutionized by Oprah. Spirituality, literature, and self-improvement are topics she focused on that reinvented her in the mid 1990s. Although unleashing a confession culture and promoting divisive self-help fads, she was criticized. She quickly becomes a benefactor to others, who generally love her for overcoming adversity.

Product Creation: Benefits of Your Product
You should start to write a well understood description of the product you have in mind. What do you want to give to your customers and what are your expectations for your product? What will it teach and what problems will it solve? Write down the benefits that your product provides so that you can have a clear picture in your head as to how you want to design and present your product. You can't go wrong after doing your market research and careful planning.

Kristen's Thoughts of the Day:
I personally think that Oprah is a nice person because she gives lots of money to charities. Philanthropy is the act of donating money, goods, time, or effort to support a charitable cause, usually over an extended period of time and in regard to a defined objective.

Daddy's Thoughts of the Day:
Many people believe that the choices they make in life have a consequence, good or bad. If you do good things, nine times out of ten good things will happen. And the reverse is equally the same. If you do bad things or make bad decisions, you will get a negative response in life. This is based on study of this Bible verse **Galatians 6:7**
"Do not be deceived; God is not mocked [fooled], for whatsoever a man soweth, that shall he also reap."

I try to get my children to understand what a seed is and how to sow it, so I take them to church and listen to our pastor speak on that topic. We listen to his "sowing and reaping programs" on CD so that we can listen and study at home. Your most valued treasure should be passed down to your kids in the form of writings, pictures, videos, etc, which is one reason King Industries has been formed.

 In response to Oprah's aforementioned quote, which we also studied during this hour, I agree. I never want them to mold themselves around standards and stereotypes. I want them to like whatever they like and do whatever it is they want to do. I don't want them not to do something because not enough African Americans are doing it, or to do something because a lot of African Americans are doing it. An example is country music. I don't want them not to like country music just because it's not popular within the African American Community. If they just don't like it, that's fine. Not to like something simply because it was created by Asian Americans, African Americans or European Americans is stupidity. That's not acceptable to me. We are human first, then African Americans.

As our study for the day comes to an end, we define and study our definition word for the day which is Discipline, defined as: 1: punishment 2.obsolete: instruction 3: a field of study 4: training that corrects, molds, or perfects the mental faculties or moral character 5 a: control gained by enforcing obedience or order b: orderly or prescribed conduct or pattern of behavior c: self-control

Definition number 4 is the one we will focus on: Training that corrects, molds, or perfects the mental faculties or moral character of a person. Being a parent, I feel as though I must do my best to discipline my children for the future because they are the future, and I want them to have the best future they can possibly have. For this reason, we take steps to help with the process, like the creation of a Rites of Passage Program, the publishing of our family book, and starting different businesses that they will have the option of managing once they are ready.

I want to teach Kristen that the color of your skin doesn't matter anymore and we can't use that as an excuse. It's now about the person you chose to become. We have been free to choose our life, even when we weren't free. Like Madam C. J. Walker and others. When I first read about this lady I was amazed by how much she accomplished during those times. It was a beautiful story that I shared with my kids, and was inspired to start Kribre.com Breon's Rites of Passage. Her goal was to start a beauty supply company and create the products.

I like Oprah's quote here, culture and understanding of one another is more important than the outside color of a person's skin. Find out who that person within is and you have found a gem. Once that person has been found, you then can change anything in your reality by thinking all day long on your goals. Program your thoughts and mind to achieve your goals. The way to change our thinking is through discipline. We must discipline ourselves so that we can pass this knowledge of self responsibility to our youth.

King Industries does this through its structure of prayer and meditation. We have to use some measure of discipline in order to complete the program. It states that discipline can be a program or training that corrects, molds, or perfects the mental faculties or moral character. Discipline is like our fuel. This is another component or aspect of character we need in our lives. As an adult we have to be disciplined to be an example for our kids. In creating a business a certain measure of discipline you must apply. We record each child's experience and they remember that they completed something that took time and effort. A certain measure of experience and discipline goes into completing the program.

Day 6:
Finding Material
Monday April 14, 2008

Daily Meditation: Morning and Evening (6:00-6:10am) and (4:30-4:40pm)
Mathew 6:6
"But when you pray, go into your room and shut the door and pray to your Father
who is in secret; and your Father who sees in secret will reward you."

MINDFUL MONDAY

As we return back to our regular schedule, keep in mind our experiences and the
mistakes we have made. Create new opportunities and new approaches to
situations we don't understand. Relax and think calmly on things that puzzle us.
Ask for clarity and look for the answer. Seek always to make better choices than
before. Be aware of what we think, do, and speak so that we can live a life that
keeps us in the place of peace.

"Genius is one percent inspiration, and ninety nine percent perspiration."
— Thomas Edison

Definition Word: self-esteem
1. A confidence and satisfaction in oneself: self-respect

5:00 – 6:00
Book Study:

Thomas Edison

6:30 – 7:00pm
Writing Section: In this section we will study and learn about Thomas Edison for
thirty minutes, define the words we don't know or understand, and study product
creation.

On February 11, 1847, Thomas Edison was born and later became an American
inventor and businessman. He was well known for his many devices and
developments that still affect life across the nation today. Edison is most famous
for his phonograph and an enduring light bulb. Edison's popularity grew, being
dubbed "The Wizard of Menlo Park" by the media. Edison is credited as being the
first inventor to relate the principles of mass production to invention.

Edison is considered one of the most creative inventors of all time, with over 1,000 U. S. patents in his name, and many patents in Germany, United Kingdom, and France, as well.

Product Creation: Finding Material

I have noticed from my research that there are certain websites that you can visit to find a market, do market research, and find a market that interest you. One of them is http://www.ehow.com and the other is http://www.bukisa.com. Keep in mind that these are "How To" websites and they can provide you with a wealth of information on anything you need. Also you can look for information in magazine articles, books, audio cassettes or DVD's. All of these are good sources of information.

Kristen's Thoughts of the Day:
Thomas Edison must have had good self-esteem because he was a successful inventor. He changed the way people live. That's something to be proud of.

Daddy's Thoughts of the Day:
You may have doubts and fears about your task. Remember that we all are called, but not many answer. I am proud of you for stepping up and co-authoring this book. Thank you for not being afraid to go through with the Rites of Passage Program. So, if you are reading it from a book, then we were successful! Rejoice and be glad in Him. According to our faith, we now know that we can accomplish our goals. We have to become that person we set out to be. With lots of study and hard work, anything is possible.

King Industries is about purpose; we teach kids to have purpose in their lives. Our purpose is to develop more self sustaining homes within our communities so we can enjoy the most simple and basic thing in life- freedom. We want to free the communities of medical bills by learning to live healthy, eliminate your utility bill because your home produces its own energy, and help create wealth for the people of that community. And a car that runs on water. Imagine that for a second, if you will? Totally free of most all expenses, right? That leaves our food. They have now learned how to create an infinite amount of food through the cloning of animals and crops. To me that spells freedom.

With an increasing amount of jobs being lost due to robots we must make a shift with the times. The time is for a revolution of technology. Study technology so that you can better prepare for what's to come. We are losing many jobs therefore we must look thirty years into the future and see in what type of society we will live. Then start looking to learn and teach your kids about what industries and fields of study they should pursue. Work on your skills daily!

1. Read every day.
2. Sharpen your imaginative skills.
3. Have a clear focus of your purpose and goals.
4. Meditate for clear concentration.
5. Control your feelings and thoughts.
6. Eat healthy and exercise regularly.

If we position ourselves right now by the time you or your kids get old enough they will know what to do to live comfortably in those future times, because you were the one that studied the future, learned from it, and adapted to it. Buy the time the shift comes you are ready for it, able to support yourself and your family in this brave new world.

Daily Meditation: Morning and Evening (6:00-6:10am) and (4:30-4:40pm)
Mathew 9:29
"According to your faith be it done unto you."

TRUSTFUL TUESDAY

Choose faith over fear and make a conscious effort to be courageous and strong. As we trust in God, the choices we make, and the people in our lives, we believe that he will see us through to the next stage of our journey. We may not know what is going on at the present moment, but pray, meditate and just trust that God will take care of us. Have no doubts or fears about trusting in what God has planned for you, regardless of whether you can see His plans or not. Until His plans are revealed, just trust.

Find out just what any people will quietly submit to and you have found out the exact measure of injustice and wrong which will be imposed upon them. These will continue till they are resisted with either words or blows, or with both. The limits of tyrants are prescribed by the endurance of those whom they oppress. In the light of these ideas, Negroes will be hunted in the North, and held and flogged in the South so long as they submit to those devilish outrages, and make no resistance, either moral or physical. Men may not get all they pay for in this world; but they must certainly pay for all they get. If we ever get free from the oppressions and wrongs heaped upon us, we must pay for their removal. We must do this by labor, by suffering, by sacrifice, and if needs be, by our lives and the lives of others.
--Frederick Douglass, Civil Disobedience Manual

Definition Word: Prosper
1: to succeed in an enterprise or activity; especially: to achieve economic success
2: to become strong and flourishing transitive verb: to cause to succeed or thrive

5:00 – 6:00
Book Study:

Frederick Douglass

6:30 – 7:00pm
Writing Section: In this section we will study and learn about Frederick Douglass for thirty minutes, define the words we don't know or understand, and study product creation.

Born Frederick Augustus Washington Bailey (February 1818 to February 1895), Douglass was an author, editor, abolitionist and a statesman and reformer. Douglass is one of the most important figures in United States and African-American history, serving as a vice presidential candidate in 1872 with Victoria Woodhull, the first female presidential candidate in the United States. They both were on the Equal Rights Party ticket. Douglass was also called, "The Lion of Anacostia", and "The Sage of Anacostia."

He stood strong in his beliefs of equality for all people, whether white or black, man or woman. One of his favorite quotes was, "I would unite with anybody to do right, with nobody to do wrong."

Frederick Douglass was born into slavery in Talbot County, Maryland, close to Hillboro. As an infant, his mother, Harriet Bailey, was sold and they were separated. When Douglass was about seven, his mother died and he went to stay with his grandmother, Betty Bailey. He didn't know his father. At twelve, his master's wife started to teach him to read. Back then, it was against the law to teach a black man to read. Her husband was furious when he found out about her teaching Douglass to read, refusing to allow that in his house. Douglass was also noted saying "if a slave learned to read, he would become dissatisfied with his condition and desire freedom."

Douglass learned to write from white children in the community and by looking at the handwriting of the men for whom he worked, he later wrote his autobiography, in 1845, Narrative of the Life of Frederick Douglass, An American Slave.

After he learned to read, he started reading everything from political newspapers to many different books with an array of topics. The youthful Douglass discovered a new dominion of thought that would lead him to question and attack slavery. Douglass, at only twelve, read the "The Columbian Orator", which he later credited with defining and describing his views on human rights and freedom.

Mr. Freeman hired Douglass from his owner, Colonel Lloyd, in 1836. He made two attempts to escape, but was unsuccessful both times.

On September 3, 1838, the more mature Douglass finally escaped the plantation by hitching a ride on a train to Havre de Grace, Maryland. He posed as a sailor and a freed black seaman gave him identification papers to board the train. By ferry, he crossed the Susquehanna River. He shortly arrived at a Wilmington, Delaware train station. He got off there and caught the steamboat to "Quaker City", Philadelphia, Pennsylvania. The entire journey to reach his destination in New York took 24 hours.

Our Bible verse we will study now: Mathew 9:29 "According to your faith be it done unto you." It's up to you, Kristen, if you want this life or not. You have to believe and take action towards your goals; no one can put in the work for you. Every man is accountable for himself. What will be the measure of your life?

Prosper
1: to succeed in an enterprise or activity; especially: to achieve economic success
2: to become strong and flourishing transitive verb: to cause to succeed or thrive.

She learned these terms and learned about money at an early age so that by the time she becomes a young adult she will be a veteran in her field. I guide her through to having a business back ground and hope that it is a good decision. Nothing we do is in vain, for it is all for the glory of God.

Douglass's quote was speaking about doing whatever it takes to survive. I want to focus on the last two sentences of his quote;

"If we ever get free from the oppressions and wrongs heaped upon us, we must pay for their removal. We must do this by labor, by suffering, by sacrifice, and if needs be, by our lives and the lives of others."

This is in reference to those times, in that time racial violence and oppression of African Americans were prevalent. Nowadays it's more about financial power and social status, education, than what you have contributed to humanity or society. Now it's about how to find and create yourself to do something you love that helps and contributes to humanity. Times have changed and we must change with it. Look towards the future for answers. All answers are here, now.

Product Creation: Market Research

If you are serious about creating a product to sell, I will give you all the resources to do so. Now, after you have a clear idea in mind about what it is you would like to create, do your market research. Specifically what information are people buying? Are they buying it online? Where do you go to create your product? How much will it cost to bring your product to market? And how long will it take to create this product?

If you haven't already begun to write your ideas and answers in your word processor, you should do so now. Statistics show that a person is more prone to take action towards something they wrote. This is a great way to get to know your product. Now you can use this information for the product section of your business plan.

Kristen's Thoughts of the Day:

Douglass prospered because he became an editor, orator, author, statesman and reformer. I think he did a very good job at that.

Daddy's Thoughts of the Day:

There are many grants out there that many of us could take advantage of. There are grants that will help you make the community green. [Grants and loans will be made available through HUD's Office of Affordable Housing Preservation (OAHP) for eligible property owners to make energy and green retrofit investments in the property, to ensure the maintenance and preservation of the property, the continued operation and maintenance of energy efficiency technologies, and the timely expenditure of funds. Physical and financial analyses of the properties will be conducted to determine the size of each grant and loan. Incentives will be made available to participating owners. The terms of the grants or loans will include continued affordability agreements. Grant and loan funds must be spent by the receiving property owner within two years. Full detail of how to apply, and grant and loan terms, will be published in a Housing Notice within 60 days of the Recovery Act being signed into law (by April 17, 2009).]

www.grant.gov

CFDA Number(s): 14.318 -- CFDA Recovery Green Retrofit

Our mission and what we plan to do is to secure one of these grants and hire the youth in the communities to fix their own communities. You can feel a sense of pride about yourself and your environment when you collectively work towards a common goal (Nia). We will use the production of this book spread the word about our cause. King Industries represents humanity and any cause for a greater good.

Robotics Engineering, Solar Energy, biomechanical are all growing industries and we should start now to train our kids in these fields. Acquiring buildings, creating science camps, classes online, whatever it takes we should provide our kids with these types of educational models. King Industries will strive to achieve the technology to have many Community Development Centers throughout the United States.

Day 8:
Proper Planning
Wednesday April 16, 2008

Daily Meditation: Morning and Evening (6:00-6:10am) and (4:30-4:40pm)
Deuteronomy 8:17
You may say to yourself, "My power and the strength of my hands have produced this wealth for me."

WONDERFUL WEDNESDAY

Throughout our day, we want to reflect on how blessed we are and how beautiful life is. We want to do our best to honor ourselves and our spirit. We want to remain humble throughout the day, never forgetting that God is not mocked. We want to remember to work hard at accomplishing our goals and increasing our talents and skills, stay focused on the task at hand so that we may excel in all that we do. Put forth effort at being the best person we can be, knowing that we are whole, together, generous, balanced, and well-rounded. We will not be afraid to let our light shine through and make a difference in the lives of others. Regardless of what the day may bring, we will remain in the position of Godliness.

Evening Meditation

5:00 – 6:00
Book Study:

W. E. B. Du Boise

Definition Word: Responsible
1. Liable to respond; likely to be called upon to answer; accountable; answerable; amenable; as, a guardian is responsible to the court for his conduct in the office.
2. Able to respond or answer for one's conduct and obligations; trustworthy, financially or otherwise; as, to have a responsible man for surety.
3. Involving responsibility; involving a degree of accountability on the part of the person concerned; as, a responsible office.

6:30 – 7:00pm
Writing Section: In this section we will study and learn about W.E.B. Du Boise for thirty minutes, define the words we don't know or understand, and study product creation.

Born William Edward Burghardt Du Bois (February 23, 1868 – August 27, 1963), there is much that can be said about W.E.B. Du Bois. He, along with Marcus Garvey, wanted to return to Africa to live and reconnect with African culture. Even though Du Bois didn't agree with Garvey's methods they both still had the same goals in mind. Du Bois finally become a naturalized citizen of Ghana in 1963, at age 95.

The work he did to create the Pan-Africanist movement was ideal for that time period, as unity was really needed. The Pan-Africanist movement was a sociopolitical world view and philosophy movement. He not only wanted to share in educating the people about the power of unity, but he also wanted to do it globally. He wanted to unite native Africans and African Americans and open their eyes to a more global economic front among all people of color. His work outlines economic growth and equal rights for all Africans, world-wide.

We then went on to talk about our Bible verse, Deuteronomy 8:17. You may say to yourself, "My power and the strength of my hands have produced this wealth for me."

Next, we have our original daily definition word, responsible:
1. Liable to respond; likely to be called upon to answer; accountable; answerable; amenable; as, a guardian is responsible to the court for his conduct in the office.
2. Able to respond or answer for one's conduct and obligations; trustworthy, financially or otherwise; as, to have a responsible man for surety.
3. Involving responsibility; involving a degree of accountability on the part of the person concerned; as, a responsible office.

Product Creation: Proper Planning
Everything in life is about taking the proper steps. What about the proper steps for success? If there was a plan for success, what would it be? Can I properly plan my life for success? A well written plan or thought-out plan, will lead you to success. But true success has to come from within. You have to want it more than anything in the world. Success comes to those who plan for success.

I can remember this saying, "If you fail to plan you plan to fail." That has always stuck with me and I will never forget it. I started dedicating more time to planning and thinking. I put the thoughts to my plans in my mind and meditate on them until they come to me, manifested. So, as you see, it takes a lot of planning and thinking about who you are and what you can create. Make sure that your product represents you as a person. That way you can feel confident and stand strong behind your products. You should start to write a well understood description of the product you have in mind. What do you want to give to your customers and what are your expectations for your product?

Kristen's Thoughts of the Day:
I think that W E B Du Bois is responsible because if he was an American civil rights activist, public intellectual, Pan-Africanist, sociologist, educator, historian, writer, editor, poet, and scholar, he would need to be. If he wasn't responsible, he would be doing his job all wrong.

Daddy's Thoughts of the Day:
I can remember this quote, by Ralph Waldo Emerson that says, "Nothing great has ever been achieved without enthusiasm." This creative force has a way of manifesting what you do towards achieving a goal or a vision. Enthusiasm is what I can hope to hold responsible for Kristen's awareness to her purpose in life. I want to start her off with goals, visions, and purpose, and for the rest of our lives we will work towards our goals with enthusiasm.

For Kristen to have deep satisfaction in what she does to achieve her goals, she has to have enthusiasm. When you allow this creative energy to flow towards your goals, visions, or just through your life, you start to change energy and frequencies. Our bodies vibrate at different rates. I wanted to show Kristen examples of vibrations and their different frequencies. We went to YouTube, a very good research tool and looked up Chlandni Patterns. This is where you would see a different design or pattern of salt vibrating on an iron plate as they change the frequency. I'm trying to get her to understand that our thoughts and emotions are vibrations of energy.

This energy can have a great impact on her life if practiced. I want to share it with her now so that she can become aware of it and learn from it. The word enthusiasm is an ancient Greek word-*en* and *theos*, which means God. The ancient Greeks had another word that related to enthusiasm called *enthousiazein which is "to be possessed by a god."* I want her to practice her meditations and learn to work with enthusiasm towards her goals in life.

Day 9:
Create Your Material to Sell
Thursday April 17, 2008

Daily Meditation: Morning and Evening (6:00-6:10am) and (4:30-4:40pm)
Mark 11:24
"Therefore I tell you, whatever you ask for in prayer, believe that you have received it, and it will be yours."

THANKFUL THURSDAY

Today we want to give thanks remembering all the things we should be thankful for. We should choose to be thankful for our experiences, good or bad, our friends, family, and most importantly our health. We should be thankful for who we are now and what we are to become. Our words of thanksgiving will be received through our prayers, our spirit, our actions and our songs. We will be still in our spirit, anxious for nothing, but thankful for all.

Evil communication corrupts good manners. I hope to live to hear that good communication corrects bad manners
--Benjamin Banneker

Definition Word: motivation
The reason or reasons for engaging in a particular behavior, especially human behavior, as studied in psychology and neurophysiology. These reasons may include basic needs such as food or a desired object, hobbies, goal, state of being, or ideal. The motivation for a behavior may also be attributed to less-apparent reasons, such as altruism or morality. According to Green motivation refers to the initiation, direction, intensity and persistence of human behavior.

5:00 – 6:00
Book Study:

Benjamin Banneker

6:30 – 7:00pm
Writing Section: In this section we will study and learn about Benjamin Banneker for thirty minutes, define the words we don't know or understand, and study product creation.

The Key of Life album written by Stevie Wonder included the song Blackman, which referenced Banneker's achievements.

Benjamin Banneker (November 9, 1731– October 9, 1806) was a free African American clockmaker, publisher, astronomer, and mathematician. It is said that his mother was a European American named Molly Banneker. Molly married one of her freed slaves and had four girls, Banneker's mother Mary being the oldest.

Robert Banneker, Benjamin's father, was a slave who built dams and watercourses that irrigated the family farm. Benjamin was taught by his grandmother to read, write, and do arithmetic. On that plantation, the Quakers changed his name to Banneker. They needed help on his parents' farm. Once old enough, he went to work on the farm and that was the end of his education for then.

At the age of 58, Banneker started studying astronomy himself. He learned to predict solar and lunar eclipses and he accumulated a wealth of information for his Benjamin Banneker's Almanac, The Sable Astronomer, is what he became known for.

Product Creation: Create Your Material to Sell
Start writing and/or creating your information. Whether it is video, a book, or recorded audio broadcast, you are now in the production state of creation. I've decided to use youtube.com as one of my marketing mediums. Just as an example, we can create a video of a real estate investor that has been in the business since 1999 and let's say she has about 18 houses. That's something like ten years of experience all on video. Write out a list of well thought out questions on how she has prospered in the market and tape the interview to market on youtube.com.

Material for creating a product is everywhere. Books you have read will give you a little bit of what direction the market is going. Almost like this can be helpful to you because that little bit of information can help you create a product for a trend that has not yet come. But you saw it, acted on it; now trust in it and bring it to market.
Always look back at your list of benefits so that you stay aware and on track with your product objectives. You promise your audience information that could help them create a product to sell online. Does your product meet your expectation of what it should provide? Carefully focus on your product and make sure that it provides all the information you described to your customers.

Kristen's Thoughts of the Day:
I think that Banneker is an interesting person. He was a free African American mathematician, astronomer, clockmaker, and publisher. Stevie Wonder wrote a song about him. It was called "Black Man."

Daddy's Thoughts of the Day:
Every opportunity is here for any to take advantage of. Make sure you know how to use the knowledge that you receive. Our people die for the lack of knowledge. Make sure you raise your kids with the knowledge, and that their friends have that same knowledge.

Every day during our forty days of the Rites of Passage Program we will make a conscientious effort to stick to the program. We will recite our prayers and keep it fresh on our minds. We will say "What things so ever ye desire, when ye pray, believe that ye receive them, and ye shall have them." Mark 11:24. Then we will take a deep breath and focus our thoughts on the words and say it again. And again..... And again.......For ten minutes. We try to imagine a deep feeling of overwhelming belief inside our bodies.

What motivates you right now will not be the same as what motivates you in the future. God is always the last resort, when God should be our first motivation. You're young and focused right now and that is where I want to continue to free your mind with the word of God. If we understand that change has to happen in our lives, why wait? Make that change now! Life is too short and precious. We only have one life to live, so live it well, happy and free.

I like how Banneker said, "Evil communication corrupts good manners. I hope to live to hear that good communication corrects bad manners." The words that come out of our mouth are the master keys to life, (Spoken Word). We would think about what we have learned in the Rites of Passage Program, and reflect on them throughout the day. You must use your knowledge throughout the day. We stay focused on His Word and what we have learned.

Day 10:
PDF Tools You Will Need for Writing
Friday April 18, 2008

Daily Meditation: Morning and Evening (6:00-6:10am) and (4:30-4:40pm)
Proverbs 8:18
With me are riches and honor, enduring wealth and prosperity.

FAITHFUL FRIDAY

Its important that we awaken to all that we are meant to be through our journey in life. Our faithfulness to ourselves will allow us to be patient in life as we become more of who we are meant to be. We should be faithful to longsuffering, bearing of pain, and dealing with trials without complaint. We should be faithful in showing self-control with others, as well as ourselves. Our faith will cause us to fight against any adversity, cause us to be focused, and fearless. Have faith throughout this day.

"Imagination is everything. It is the preview of life's coming attractions"
--Albert Einstein

Definition Word: Imagination
The ability to form mental images or to spontaneously generate images within one's own mind; it helps provide meaning to experience and understanding to knowledge; it is a fundamental facility through which people make sense of the world, and it also plays a key role in the learning process.

5:00 – 6:00
Book Study:
Albert Einstein

6:30 – 7:00pm
Writing Section: In this section we will study and learn about Albert Einstein for thirty minutes, define the words we don't know or understand, and study product creation.

Albert Einstein a German-born speculative physicist was born in March 14, 1879 and died April 18, 1955. He was well known specifically for mass-energy equivalence and his theory of relativity, E=mc2.

Einstein's many contributions to physics include his special theory of relativity, which reconciled mechanics with electromagnetism, and his general theory of relativity, which extended the principle of relativity to non-uniform motion, creating a new theory of gravitation. His other contributions include relativistic cosmology, capillary action, critical opalescence, classical problems of statistical mechanics and their application to quantum theory, an explanation of the Brownian movement of molecules, atomic transition probabilities, the quantum theory of a monatomic gas, thermal properties of light with low radiation density (which laid the foundation for the photon theory), a theory of radiation including stimulated emission, the conception of a unified field theory, and the geometrization of physics.

Einstein published over 300 scientific works and over 150 non-scientific works. Einstein is revered by the physics community and in 1999, Time magazine named him the "Person of the Century". In wider cultures, the name "Einstein" has become synonymous with genius.

In Physics, Einstein received the Nobel Prize in 1921. He received this prize "for his services to Theoretical Physics and especially for his discovery of the law of the photoelectric effect". This refers to his 1905 paper on the photoelectric effect: "On a Heuristic Viewpoint Concerning the Production and Transformation of Light", which was well supported by the experimental evidence by that time. The presentation speech began by mentioning "his theory of relativity [which had] been the subject of lively debate in philosophical circles [and] also has astrophysical implications which are being rigorously examined at the present time." (Einstein 1923) As stipulated in their 1919 divorce settlement, Einstein gave the Nobel Prize money to his first wife, Mileva Marić.

Einstein traveled to New York City in the United States for the first time on April 2, 1921. When asked where he got his scientific ideas, Einstein explained that he believed scientific work best results from an examination of physical reality and a search for underlying axioms, with consistent explanations that apply in all instances and avoid contradicting each other. He also recommended theories with results that can be quantified by research.

Product Creation: PDF Tools You Will Need for Writing

All of the products you create for text or books can easily be saved to a PDF file and can be sold as an e-book online, or sent to the local press. You can even put it in the form of a binder for trainings or seminars. Selling binders for $125 at seminars which cost me only $28 to produce is a quick and easy way to wealth. Can you start to see how product creation can benefit you as an online business?

Sometimes people ask me where I get the material for my book. Everywhere around us is knowledge. Collect it, organize it, and redistribute it. It's going to take some effort, discipline, and time but it's worth it. Most of us work and don't have the time to write a book. The hard cold truth is, you will never have enough time. And nothing will ever change unless you do something different and change it.

This is a simple way to write anything and convert files into a PDF file. Go to Docudesk.com and download your free software. This will allow you to create PDF files which will come in handy for your online sales of e-books or any other published material.

Kristen's Thoughts of the Day:

I think that people thought he had a good imagination. I think that people thought he was imagining things when he talked about his special theory of relativity.

Daddy's Thoughts of the Day:

We try to use all these concepts to create our life. For instance OWP (Our World of Prayer) was created to help stimulate our imagination while we pray. King Industries want to instill purpose with in communities through cooperative economics. What goal as a community can we imagine and work towards together? This will give people purpose. The purpose of a community is to work together. Have you ever seen that movie "The Last Samurai", I love this movie because of the discipline of the Samurai. It was a disciplined culture and they preserved their way of life. They were willing to die for their culture and what they believed in. The entire community worked together as one. They fought and died together and live in harmony as one.

Day 11:
Freelance Writing
Saturday April 19, 2008

Daily Meditation: Morning and Evening (6:00-6:10am) and (4:30-4:40pm)
Acts 6:3-4
Brothers, choose seven men from among you who are known to be full of the
Spirit and wisdom. We will turn this responsibility over to them and will give our
attention to prayer and the ministry of the word."

SUCCESSFUL SATURDAY

To have made it to Successful Saturday is truly a wonderful success. Throughout
the week we have walked by faith, renewed our minds and spirit, and have trusted
in the all powerful universe. We have maintained a wonderful character and we are
thankful for whom we are and all that we have. To remain strong and in character
throughout the week is truly defined as a success.

If you succumb to the temptation of using violence in the struggle, unborn
generations will be the recipients of a long and duologue night of bitterness and
your chief legacy to the future will be an endless reign of meaningless chaos.
--Martin Luther King, Jr.

Definition Word: persistence
To persist in a state, enterprise, or undertaking in spite of counterinfluences,
opposition, or discouragement

5:00 – 6:00
Book Study:

Martin Luther King Jr.

6:30 – 7:00pm
Writing Section: In this section we will study and learn about Rev. Dr. Martin
Luther King Jr. for thirty minutes, define the words we don't know or understand,
and study product creation.

Martin Luther King, Jr. (January 15, 1929 – April 4, 1968) was one of the pivotal leaders of the American civil rights movement. King was a Baptist minister, one of the few leadership roles available to black men at the time. He became a civil rights activist early in his career. He led the Montgomery Bus Boycott (1955–1956) and helped found the Southern Christian Leadership Conference (1957), serving as its first president. His efforts led to the 1963 March on Washington, where King delivered his "I Have a Dream" speech. Here he raised public consciousness of the civil rights movement and established himself as one of the greatest orators in U.S. history. In 1964, King became the youngest person to receive the Nobel Peace Prize for his efforts to end segregation and racial discrimination through civil disobedience and other non-violent means.

King was assassinated on April 4, 1968, in Memphis, Tennessee. He was posthumously awarded the Presidential Medal of Freedom by President Jimmy Carter in 1977. Martin Luther King, Jr. Day was established as a national holiday in the United States in 1986. In 2004, King was posthumously awarded a Congressional Gold Medal.

Martin Luther King, Jr., was born on January 15, 1929, in Atlanta, Georgia. He was the son of the Reverend Martin Luther King, Sr. and Alberta Williams King. King's father was born "Michael King", and Martin Luther King, Jr. was initially named "Michael King, Jr.", until 1935, when "his father changed both of their names to Martin to honor the German Protestant (Martin Luther)." He had an older sister, Willie Christine (born September 11, 1927) and a younger brother, Alfred Daniel (July 30, 1930 – July 1, 1969). King sang with his church choir at the 1939 Atlanta premiere of the movie Gone with the Wind. He entered Morehouse College at age fifteen, skipping his ninth and twelfth high school grades without formally graduating. In 1948, he graduated from Morehouse with a Bachelor of Arts (B.A.) degree in sociology, and enrolled in Crozer Theological Seminary in Chester, Pennsylvania, from which graduated with a Bachelor of Divinity (B.D.) degree in 1951. In September 1951, King began doctoral studies in systematic theology at Boston University and received his Doctor of Philosophy (Ph.D.) on June 5, 1955. In 1954, at age 25, King became pastor of the Dexter Avenue Baptist Church in Montgomery, Alabama.

Product Creation: Freelance Writing

This is a curriculum and a must do for members going through the program. You may want to get into freelance writing. This is a good way to get your skills up to par. You can also gain more exposure for your product by writing about it and explaining the benefits. Keep in mind that if you are creating a product, you are entering the ecommerce market and you will have to establish yourself. Freelance writing is a good place to start. Start by creating articles to submit online as this will get your foot in the door. I have found that Ezinearticles.com is a good website to write and create your-self as a freelance writer.

Kristen's Thoughts of the Day:
Martin Luther King was one of the most pivotal leaders of the American civil rights movement. His speech "I Have a Dream" is now one of the greatest speeches ever. Well that's what I think about it.

Daddy's Thoughts of the Day:
Kristen's Rites of Passage is a program that encourages members to write their imaginations and future goals in a book after each day of the program. Through the Rites of Passage Program we share the knowledge and power of Command. We demonstrate the law of command by willingly, and consciously meditating to bring our goals into existence, making them a reality.

Day 12:
Resell Rights
Sunday April 20, 2008

Daily Meditation: Morning and Evening (6:00-6:10am) and (4:30-4:40pm)
Ecclesiastes 3:1
There is a time for everything, and a season for every activity under heaven:

SOULFUL SUNDAY

We should look to overflow our spirits with something good. A good word produces a good feeling. Today, we should remain in the place of peace, filling our soul with the joy and happiness from the word. Surround yourself with people of like faith and celebrate life. Remember to enjoy life on this day. Synagogue, temple, mosque, or church, whatever your faith we should be humane to one another. Seek to fill yourself with an empowering word that will keep you motivated and inspired with the love you see all around us.

Musicians don't retire; they stop when there's no more music in them.
--Louis Armstrong

Definition Word: loyalty
1 a: the quality or state of being faithful b: accuracy in details: exactness

5:00 – 6:00
Book Study:

Louis Armstrong

6:30 – 7:00pm
Writing Section: In this section we will study and learn about Louis Armstrong for thirty minutes, define the words we don't know or understand, and study product creation.

Louis Armstrong (August 4, 1901 – July 6, 1971), nicknamed Satchmo and Pops, was an American jazz trumpeter and singer.

Armstrong was a charismatic, innovative performer whose improvised soloing was the main influence for a fundamental change in jazz, shifting its focus from collective improvisation to the solo player and improvised soloing. One of the most famous jazz musicians of the 20th century, he was first known as a cornet player, then as a trumpet player, and toward the end of his career he was best known as a vocalist and became one of the most influential jazz singers.

Product Creation: Resell Rights

Another good way to break into the industry of e-commerce is to buy the resell rights to e-books. You can do this simple and easy by going to http://www.impress-a-print.com. This will allow you to pick your subject of e-books you want to sell. It's then your product to resell as your own.

You would then follow the steps outlined for creating your website and market your product online. Resale right gives you access to thousands of e-books you can personalize as your own, great for beginners.

Kristen's Thoughts of the Day:
From the stories I hear about Louis Armstrong I would like to hear him play. The stories say that Louis Armstrong was one of the most famous jazz musicians of the 20th century.

Daddy's Thoughts of the Day:
I want her to be loyal to her work, and see it as being…life, a part of who she is. Right now, she doesn't fully understand that the project she is working on through King will advance her career as a writer. She doesn't even know whether she wants to be a writer or not, but at least she would have developed that skill and created that opportunity for herself. So, it's her choice what she wants to do for the rest of her life; I'm just trying to give her as many options as possible.

"What you decide on will be done, and light will shine on your ways."—Job 22:28

"I tell you the truth, if anyone says to this mountain, 'Go, throw yourself into the sea,' and does not doubt in his heart but believes that what he says will happen, it will be done for him."—Mark 11:23

Day 13:
Writing Special Reports
Monday April 21, 2008

Daily Meditation: Morning and Evening (6:00-6:10am) and (4:30-4:40pm)
John 12:44
Then Jesus cried out, "When a man believes in me, he does not believe in me only, but in the one who sent me."

MINDFUL MONDAY

As we return back to our regular schedule, keep in mind our experiences and the mistakes we have made. Create new opportunities and new approaches to situations we don't understand. Relax and think calmly on things that puzzle us. Ask for clarity and look for the answer. Seek always to make better choices than before. Be aware of what we think, do, and speak so that we can live a life that keeps us in the place of peace.

Education is the most powerful weapon which you can use to change the world.
--Nelson Mandela

Definition Word: Dedication
1: an act or rite of dedicating to a divine being or to a sacred use 2: a devoting or setting aside for a particular purpose 3: a name and often a message prefixed to a literary, musical, or artistic production in tribute to a person or cause 4: self-sacrificing devotion <her dedication to the cause> 5: a ceremony to mark the official completion or opening of something (as a building)

5:00 – 6:00
Book Study:

Nelson Mandela
6:30 – 7:00pm
Writing Section: In this section we will study and learn about Nelson Mandela for thirty minutes, define the words we don't know or understand, and study product creation.

Nelson Rolihlahla Mandela IPA, born (July 18, 1918), is a former President of South Africa, the first to be elected in fully representative democratic elections. Before his presidency, Mandela was an anti-apartheid activist and leader of the African National Congress and its armed wing Umkhonto we Sizwe. He spent 27 years in prison, much of it on Robben Island, on convictions for crimes that included sabotage committed while he spearheaded the struggle against apartheid.

Among opponents of apartheid in South Africa and internationally, he became a symbol of freedom and equality, while the apartheid government and nations sympathetic to it condemned him and the ANC as communists and terrorists (the United States still lists the ANC as a terrorist organization, though the United States Congress is considering removing the designation).

Following his release from prison on February 11, 1990, his switch to a policy of reconciliation and negotiation helped lead the transition to multi-racial democracy in South Africa. Since the end of apartheid, he has been widely praised, even by former opponents.

Mandela has received more than one hundred awards over four decades, most notably the Nobel Peace Prize in 1993. He is currently a celebrated elder statesman who continues to voice his opinion on topical issues. In South Africa he is often known as Madiba, an honorary title adopted by elders of Mandela's clan. The title has come to be synonymous with Nelson Mandela.

Mandela has frequently credited Mahatma Gandhi for being a major source of inspiration in his life, both for the philosophy of non-violence and for facing adversity with dignity.

Mandela belongs to a cadet branch of the Thembu dynasty which (nominally) reigns in the Transkeian Territories of the Union of South Africa's Cape Province. He was born in the small village of Mvezo in the district of Umtata, the Transkei capital. His great-grandfather was Ngubengcuka (died 1832), the Inkosi Enkhulu or King of the Thembu people, who were eventually subjected to British colonial rule. One of the king's sons, named Mandela, became Nelson's grandfather and the source of his surname. However, being only the Inkosi's child by a wife of the Ixhiba clan (the so-called "Left-Hand House"), the descendants of his branch of the royal family was not eligible to succeed to the Thembu throne. His father, Gadla Henry Mphakanyiswa (1880–1928), was nonetheless designated chief of the town of Mvezo. Upon alienating the colonial authorities, however, he was deprived of his position, and moved his family to Qunu. Gadla remained, however, a member of the Inkosi's Privy Council, and was instrumental in the ascension to the Thembu throne of Jongintaba Dalindyebo, who would later return this favor by informally adopting Mandela upon Gadla's death. Mandela's father had four wives, with whom he fathered a total of thirteen children (four boys and nine girls). Mandela was born to Gadla's third wife ('third' by a complex royal ranking system), Nosekeni Fanny, daughter of Nkedama of the Mpemvu Xhosa clan, the dynastic Right Hand House, in whose umzi or homestead Mandela spent much of his childhood. His given name Rolihlahla means "to pull a branch of a tree", or more colloquially, "troublemaker".

Product Creation: Writing Special Reports

Along with the short and sweet articles you write to help promote your products, you should learn to create special reports as well. A report, is sometimes called a folio, which is a written document specialized for a certain reader or for certain interest. It should be precise information of value to your customer. Why Special Reports are good? For one, they are very inexpensive to produce. And, it targets a certain need of the consumer.

Let's just say, you have a report that explains exactly how to get a $5000 government grant to help get out of debt. Would this be valuable to some people? How much would you pay for information like this? Would you pay $15? It may have only taken minutes to write with no overhead cost, other than a computer. You can sell them one at a time with no inventory to worry about or you can sell according to orders received.

A special report is a good way to start your information empire without having to pay a large overhead. Books and other informational DVDs or CDs have to be ordered in bulk, so you have to invest cash up-front. With books, you have to invest much more time and effort to produce. Reports are only about one to two pages long; therefore, less time, money and effort is invested.

First, research the market to find out what you should write about. Google is a great place to start. Magazine articles and advertisements will always let you know what people are buying and what information they want. Like moneymaking information. Do you think this is a thriving market? You bet it is! People are more likely to pay $15 to get a special report than to pay $24 dollars for a book with only one relevant chapter.

Set a goal and meditate on achieving that goal for your publishing empire. Remember that to write a special report, all it takes is research, writing, and editing. Stay focused on your schedule. Self discipline is a must and before long you will have written the makings of a self published book. By producing a special report every month, at the end of the year you are now ready to publish all of your reports into one book. Now you have 12 special reports and a book you can sell for years, generating an income. Rome wasn't built in a day. Slowly and patiently establish yourself in the industry where you want to create your products.

Kristen's Thoughts of the Day:
I've learned that Nelson Mandela was a former President of South Africa, the first to be elected in fully representative democratic elections. He wasn't always a president. Before he was a president he was an anti-apartheid activist and leader of the African National Congress. That's pretty cool.

Daddy's Thoughts of the Day:
We use Nelson Mandela because he was a very dedicated person; you have to be a dedicated person to stop Apartheid in South Africa. Now that Kristen has learned of a person that showed tremendous strength to overcome the odds, she needs to use these stories of real people and apply their courage and strength to her life and struggles.

Day 14:
Self-Publishing
Tuesday April 22, 2008

Daily Meditation: Morning and Evening (6:00-6:10am) and (4:30-4:40pm)
Mark 11:25
"And when you stand praying, if you hold anything against anyone, forgive him, so that your father in heaven may forgive you your sins."

TRUSTFUL TUESDAY

Today choose faith over fear and make a conscious effort to be courageous and strong. As we trust in God, the choices we make, and the people in our lives, believe that he will see us through to the next stage of our journey. We may not know what is going on at the present moment, but pray, meditate and just trust that God will take care of us. Have no doubts or fears about trusting in what God has planned for you, regardless of if you can see his plans or not. Until his plans are revealed, just trust.

Life isn't about finding yourself. Life is about creating yourself.
--George Bernard Shaw

Definition Word: Vigor
 1: active bodily or mental strength or force 2: active healthy well-balanced growths especially of plants 3: intensity of action or effect: force 4: effective legal status

5:00 – 6:00
Book Study:

George Bernard Shaw

6:30 – 7:00pm
Writing Section: In this section we will study and learn about George Bernard Shaw for thirty minutes, define the words we don't know or understand, and study product creation.

George Bernard Shaw (26 July 1856 – 2 November 1950) was an Irish playwright. Born in Dublin, he moved to London at the age of twenty and lived in England for the remainder of his life.

Although Shaw's first profitable writing was music and literary criticism, his talent was for drama, and during his career he authored more than sixty plays. Nearly all of his writings deal sternly with prevailing social problems, but are leavened by a vein of comedy to make their stark themes more palatable. Shaw examined education, marriage, religion, government, health care, and class privilege and found them all defective, but his desire was most aroused by the exploitation of the working class; his writings seldom fail to censure that abuse. An ardent socialist, Shaw wrote many brochures and speeches for the Fabian Society. He became an accomplished orator in the furtherance of its causes, which included gaining equal political rights for men and women, alleviating abuses of the working class, rescinding private ownership of productive land, and promoting healthful lifestyles.

He is the only person to have been awarded both the Nobel Prize for Literature (1925) and an Oscar (1938). These were for his contributions to literature and for his work on the film Pygmalion, respectively. Shaw would have refused his Nobel Prize outright, because he had no desire for public honors, but accepted it at his wife's behest: she considered it a tribute to Ireland. He did reject the monetary award, requesting it be used to finance translation of Swedish books to English.

George Bernard Shaw was born in Dublin in 1856 to George Carr Shaw (1814–1885), an unsuccessful grain merchant and sometime civil servant, and Lucinda Elizabeth Shaw, née Gurly (1830–1913), a professional singer. He had two sisters, Lucinda Frances (1853–1920), a singer of musical comedy and light opera, and Elinor Agnes (1854–1876). George briefly attended the Wesleyan Connexional School, a grammar school operated by the Methodist New Connexion, before moving to a private school near Dalkey and then transferring to Dublin's Central Model School. He ended his formal education at the Dublin English Scientific and Commercial Day School. He harbored a lifelong animosity toward schools and teachers, saying, "Schools and schoolmasters, as we have them today, are not popular as places of education and teachers, but rather prisons and turnkeys in which children are kept to prevent them disturbing and chaperoning their parents."

Shaw expressed this attitude in the astringent prologue to "Cashel Byron's Profession" where young Byron's educational experience is a fictionalized description of Shaw's own schooldays. Later he painstakingly detailed the reasons for his aversion to formal education in his Treatise on Parents and Children. In brief, he considered the standardized curricula useless, deadening to the spirit and stifling to the intellect. He particularly deplored the use of corporal punishment, which was prevalent in his time.

When his mother left home and followed her voice teacher, George Vandeleur Lee, to London, Shaw was almost sixteen years old. His sisters accompanied their mother but Shaw remained in Dublin with his father, first as a reluctant pupil, then as a clerk in an estate office. He worked efficiently, albeit discontentedly, for several years. In 1876, Shaw joined his mother's London household. She, Vandeleur Lee, and his sister Lucy, provided him with a pound a week while he frequented public libraries and the British Museum reading room where he studied earnestly and began writing novels. He earned his allowance by ghost-writing Vandeleur Lee's music column, which appeared in the London Hornet. His novels were rejected, however, so his literary earnings remained negligible until 1885, when he became self-supporting as a critic of the arts.

Influenced by his reading, he became a dedicated Socialist and a charter member of the Fabian Society, a middle class organization established in 1884 to promote the gradual spread of socialism by peaceful means. In the course of his political activities he met Charlotte Payne-Townshend, an Irish heiress and fellow Fabian; they married in 1898. In 1906 the Shaws moved into a house, now called Shaw's Corner, in Ayot St Lawrence, a small village in Hertfordshire; it was to be their home for the remainder of their lives, although they also maintained a residence at 29 Fitzroy Square in London. During his final years Shaw enjoyed tending to the grounds at Shaw's Corner. His death, at 94, from renal failure, was precipitated by injuries incurred by falling while pruning a tree. His ashes, mixed with those of his wife, were scattered along the footpaths and around the statue of Saint Joan in their garden.

Shaw's plays were first performed in the 1890s. By the end of the decade he was an established playwright. He wrote sixty-three plays and his output as novelist, critic, pamphleteer, essayist and private correspondent was prodigious. He is known to have written more than 250,000 letters. Along with Fabian Society members Sidney Webb and Beatrice Webb and Graham Wallas, Shaw founded the London School of Economics and Political Science in 1895 with funding provided by private philanthropy, including a bequest of £20,000 from Henry Hunt Hutchinson to the Fabian Society. One of the libraries at the LSE is named in Shaw's honor; it contains collections of his papers and photographs.

Product Creation: Self-Publishing

Self publishing is not as easy as you may think. Often, people are working day jobs and do not have the time to come home and write. The bottom line is, if you can't find the time to research your ideas of subjects to write about then you can't find the time to write it. To become a successful self publisher, you must write. You have to write articles, books, reports, etc. in order to make money in this field. Now, there are other ways of producing. If you like to talk, you can buy software that will print every word you speak into your word processor. Now you can speak most of your products.

Also, video is popular, and always has been, a very good means to create a product. Self publishing is easy if you can find just two hours out of your day to work on building your empire. I say empire because with the amount of money you will make, you will create an "empire" of informational products to sell.

Kristen's Thoughts of the Day:

George Bernard Shaw was an Irish playwright. He died at the age of 94 in November 2, 1950. He was born in July 26, 1856. Guess what, when he was 20 he lived in England for the rest of his life. He had a cool life.

Daddy's Thoughts of the Day:

I started reading the dictionary to my kids at a very early age and one of our words we learned was "vigor" at the age of three. That molding was instilled in them at an early age and it never left them. Both of my daughters are strong and smart little girls with honors in school. We already have a college in mind, H.U. baby! Howard University is the place for them. We will travel to the college and visit during the summer of their high school years. With continued vigor towards their learning, they will go far in life and I will be proud of them. No matter what they choose, I just hope that it's doing something for the improvement of mankind!

Daily Meditation: Morning and Evening (6:00-6:10am) and (4:30-4:40pm)
John 14: 20
On that day you will realize that I am in my Father, and you are in me, and I am in you.

WONDERFUL WEDNESDAY

Throughout our day, we want to reflect on how blessed we are and how beautiful life is. We want to do our best to honor ourselves and our spirit. We want to remain humble throughout the day, never forgetting that God is not mocked. We want to remember to work hard at accomplishing our goals and increasing our talents and skills, stay focused on the task at hand so that we may excel in all that we do. Put forth effort at being the best person we can be, knowing that we are whole, together, generous, balanced, and well-rounded. We will not be afraid to let our light shine through and make a difference in the lives of others. Regardless of what the day may bring, we will remain in the position of Godliness.

A rooster crows only when it sees the light. Put him in the dark and he'll never crow. I have seen the light and I'm crowing.
--Muhammad Ali

Definition Word: Strength
The quality or state of being strong: capacity for exertion or endurance 2: power to resist force: solidity, toughness 3: power of resisting attack: impregnability 4 a: legal, logical, or moral force b: a strong attribute or inherent asset. 5 a: degree of potency of effect or of concentration.

5:00 – 6:00
Book Study:

Muhammad Ali

6:30 – 7:00pm
Writing Section: In this section we will study and learn about Muhammad Ali for thirty minutes, define the words we don't know or understand, and study product creation.

Muhammad Ali (born Cassius Marcellus Clay Jr. on January 17, 1942) is a retired American boxer and former three-time World Heavyweight Champion and winner of an Olympic Light-heavyweight gold medal. In 1999, Ali was crowned "Sportsman of the Century" by Sports Illustrated and the BBC.

Ali was born in Louisville, Kentucky. He was named after his father, Cassius Marcellus Clay Sr., who was named for the 19th century abolitionist and politician Cassius Clay. Ali changed his name after joining the Nation of Islam in 1964, subsequently converted to Sunni Islam in 1975 and then Sufism.

Product Creation: Get Your ISBN
All self publishers need to know how to obtain their own ISBN (International Standard Book Number) for their products. For every product you create, you will need an ISBN. You can obtain your ISBN in blocks of ten or one at a time. To obtain your numbers, go to: http://myidentifiers.com/. I like this site because you can get your ISBN, as well as your barcode together, and it is less expensive for new publishers trying to create their own material.

Kristen's Thoughts of the Day:
Muhammad Ali is a retired American boxer and former three-time World Heavyweight Champion and winner of an Olympic Light-heavyweight gold medal. He would say he was the greatest when he was boxing. I think that he was a strong person.

Daddy's Thoughts of the Day:
I had to give them a quick synopsis about Ali, and all the lessons one could learn from this man during his time. Strength, determination, honor, shall I go on? I mean, what more can you say about the man who was "The Greatest"? Even though he didn't know who he was at the time, he continued to press forward and before he knew it the molding of greatness was complete. Now, he could see himself completely after being unaware of what extent or caliber of man he would become.

Day 16:
Bar Code Your Products
Thursday April 24, 2008

Daily Meditation: Morning and Evening (6:00-6:10am) and (4:30-4:40pm)
2 Corinthians 8:9
For you know the grace of our Lord Jesus Christ, that though He was rich, yet for your sakes He became poor, so that you through His poverty might become rich.

THANKFUL THURSDAY

We want to give thanks, remembering all the things we should be thankful for. We should choose to be thankful for our experiences, good or bad, our friends, family, and most importantly our health. We should be thankful for who we are now and what we are to become. Our words of thanksgiving will be received through our prayers, our spirit, our actions and our songs. We will be still in our spirit, anxious for nothing, but thankful for all.

A man in debt is so far a slave.
--Ralph Waldo Emerson

Definition Word: Principles
1 a: a comprehensive and fundamental law, doctrine, or assumption b (1): a rule or code of conduct (2): habitual devotion to right principles. C: the laws or facts of nature underlying the working of an artificial device2: a primary source : origin 3 a: an underlying faculty or endowment. b: an ingredient (as a chemical) that exhibits or imparts a characteristic quality for capitalized Christian Science : a divine principle : god— In principle: with respect to fundamentals

5:00 – 6:00
Book Study:

Ralph Waldo Emerson

6:30 – 7:00pm
Writing Section: In this section we will study and learn about Ralph Waldo Emerson for thirty minutes, define the words we don't know or understand, and study product creation.

Ralph Waldo Emerson (25 May 1803 – 27 April 1882) and his teachings directly influenced the growing New Thought movement of the mid 1800s. Emerson gradually moved away from the religious and social beliefs of his contemporaries, formulating and expressing the philosophy of Transcendentalism in his 1836 essay, Nature. As a result of this ground breaking work he gave a speech entitled "The American Scholar" in 1837, which Oliver Wendell Holmes Sr. considered to be America's "Intellectual Declaration of Independence". Emerson once said "Make the most of yourself, for that is all there is of you.

Emerson was considered one of the great orators of the time. Emerson's enthusiasm and respect for his audience enraptured crowds. His support for abolitionism late in life created controversy, and at times he was subject to abuse from crowds while speaking on the topic; however this was not always the case. When asked to sum up his work, he said his central doctrine was "the infinitude of the private man."

Product Creation: Bar Code Your Products

Bar Code Services are done by Bowker Publishing Services at http://www.bowkerbarcode.com/barcode/, where you have to register your bar code so that it can be placed into their database. I would recommend you take advantage of all the services they provide. There are many different services being advertised on their website. For instance, www.PubEasy.com is a website that gives you access to order placement, tracks orders, shows prices and titles, all online. It connects with other publishers, distributors and wholesalers. You also have other sites as they are affiliated with that you should learn more about as you get more involved in product creation or writing your materials.

Kristen's Thoughts of the Day:

He was an American essayist, philosopher, poet, and leader of the Transcendentalist movement in the early 19th century. His teachings directly influenced the growing New Thought movement of the mid 1800s. He did so many things.

Daddy's Thoughts of the Day:

As we learn about different principles to incorporate into our own family, we would want our kids to remain faithful to what we have taught them. I want her to see the importance of standing strong for something noble an honorable instead of falling for the foolish illusions of the world. The lies and all the types of manipulation strategies people play (head games). The opportunity of wealth is always there. Our focus is not on wealth but on living by our principles daily, never to forget what we stand for and who we are.

Daily Meditation: Morning and Evening (6:00-6:10am) and (4:30-4:40pm)
Proverbs 13:4
"The sluggard craves and gets nothing, but the desires of the diligent are fully satisfied"

FAITHFUL FRIDAY

It's important that we awaken to all that we are meant to be through our journey in life. Our faithfulness to ourselves will allow us to be patient in life as we become more of who we are meant to be. We should be faithful to longsuffering, bearing of pain, and dealing with trials without complaint. We should be faithful in showing self-control with others, as well as ourselves. Our faith will cause us to fight against any adversity, cause us to be focused, and fearless. Have faith throughout this day.

Definition Word: Morals
1. a comprehensive and fundamental law, doctrine, or assumption b (1): a rule or code of conduct (2): habitual devotion to right principles c: the laws or facts of nature underlying the working of an artificial device 2: a primary source, origin 3: an underlying faculty or endowment. b: an ingredient (as a chemical) that exhibits or imparts a characteristic quality 4. Christian Science: a divine principle: God— in principle: With respect to fundamentals.

5:00 – 6:00
Book Study:

Dr. Cornell West

6:30 – 7:00pm
Writing Section: In this section we will study and learn about Dr. cornell West for thirty minutes, define the words we don't know or understand, and study product creation.

West was born (June 2, 1953) in Tulsa, Oklahoma. The grandson of a preacher, West marched as a young man in civil rights demonstrations and organized protests demanding black studies courses at his high school. West later wrote that, in his youth, he admired "the sincere black militancy of Malcolm X, the defiant rage of the Black Panther Party [...] and the livid black theology of James Cone."

After graduating from John F. Kennedy High School in Sacramento, California, where he served as president of his high school class, he enrolled at Harvard University at age 17. He took classes from philosophers Robert Nozick and Stanley Cavell and graduated in three years, magna cum laude in Near Eastern Languages and Civilization in 1973. He was determined to press the university and its intellectual traditions into the service of his political agendas and not the other way around: to have its educational agendas imposed on him. "Owing to my family, church, and the black social movements of the 1960s," he says, "I arrived at Harvard unashamed of my African, Christian, and militant de-colonized outlooks. More pointedly, I acknowledged and accented the empowerment of my black styles, mannerisms, and viewpoints, my Christian values of service, love, humility, and struggle, and my anti-colonial sense of self-determination for oppressed people and nations around the world."

He earned a Ph.D. in 1980 from Princeton, where he was influenced by Richard Rorty's pragmatism. He later published his dissertation (completed in 1980) as The Ethical Dimensions of Marxist Thought.

In his mid-twenties, he returned to Harvard as a Du Bois fellow before becoming an assistant professor at Union Theological Seminary in New York City. In 1985 he went to Yale Divinity School in what eventually became a joint appointment in American studies. While at Yale, he participated in campus protests for a clerical union and divestment from apartheid South Africa, one of which resulted in his being arrested and jailed. As punishment, the university administration cancelled his leave for Spring 1987, leading him to commute between Yale (where he was teaching two classes) and the University of Paris.

He then returned to Union and taught at Haverford College for one year before going to Princeton to become a professor of religion and director of the Program in African American Studies, which he revitalized in cooperation with such scholars as novelist Toni Morrison. He served as director of the program from 1988 to 1994.

He then accepted an appointment as professor of African-American studies at Harvard University, with a joint appointment at the Divinity School. West taught one of the university's most popular courses, an introductory class on African-American studies. In 1998 he was appointed the first Alphonse Fletcher University Professor, a position that placed him among a select two dozen professors at the university and freed him from departmental boundaries. West used this freedom to teach not only in African-American studies but in divinity, religion, and in philosophy (where he co-taught a course on American pragmatism with Hilary Putnam).

In 2001, after a public row with Harvard president Lawrence Summers, West returned to Princeton, where he has taught since. The recipient of more than 20 honorary degrees and an American Book Award, he is a longtime member of the Democratic Socialists of America, for which he now serves as Honorary Chair. He is also a co-chair of the Tikkun Community and the Network of Spiritual Progressives. West is a board member of the International Bridges to Justice, among others. West is also much sought-after as a speaker, blurb-writer, and honorary chair.

Critics, most notably The New Republic literary editor Leon Wieseltier, have charged him with opportunism, crass showmanship and lack of scholarly seriousness. West remains a widely cited scholar in the popular press, in African-American studies, and in studies of black theology, although his work as an academic philosopher has been almost completely ignored (with the exception of his early history of American pragmatism, The American Evasion of Philosophy).

Dr. Cornell West is a member of Alpha Phi Alpha Fraternity, Inc, the oldest fraternity established for African American undergraduates.

Product Creation: Copyright Your Work
For my products I've decided not to use outside source information other than the Bible and the free encyclopedia. Make sure to copyright your work; products, websites, audio, video, etc.... it's yours, so you should protect it. Copyright all material. At copyright.gov you can file all of your material for $35.

Kristen's Thoughts of the Day:
I think that he is a very smart man that will accomplish a lot.

Daddy's Thoughts of the Day:
As a man, I can now appreciate why a single mother, my mom, had to be a strict disciplinarian and I thank her for instilling in me the will to work hard. "Laziness will get you nowhere", and "You will constantly look to others for help, if you don't take control of your own life", or "If you want something done.....do it yourself". All these sayings, I have experienced...lived....and learned from. Do not ever become comfortable with going without. Don't settle for less. If you need something, go and get it yourself. If you need to learn something to get it, then learn it. If you need money to get it, then make it. Use your creative artistic energy, strength, and principles to propel you towards what you need and want. Have faith and believe that you have it already and it is........YOURS!

Day 18:
Registering Your Domain Name
Saturday April 26, 2008

Daily Meditation: Morning and Evening (6:00-6:10am) and (4:30-4:40pm)
Hosea 4:6
"My people are destroyed for lack of knowledge. Because you have rejected knowledge, I also reject you as my priest. Since; because you have ignored the law of your God, I also will ignore your children".

SUCCESSFUL SATURDAY
To have made it to Successful Saturday is truly a wonderful success. Throughout the week we have walked by faith, renewed our minds and spirit, and have trusted in the all powerful universe. We have maintained a wonderful character and we are thankful for whom we are and all that we have. To remain strong and in character throughout the week is truly defined as a success.

"There is no royal flower-strewn path to success. And if there is, I have not found it, for if I have accomplished anything in life it is because I have been willing to work-hard."
--Madam C. J. Walker

Definition Word: Values
1: a fair return or equivalent in goods, services, or money for something exchanged
2: the monetary worth of something: market price3: relative worth, utility, or importance.

5:00 – 6:00
Book Study:

Madam C. J. Walker

6:30 – 7:00pm
Writing Section: In this section we will study and learn about Madam C. J. Walker for thirty minutes, define the words we don't know or understand, and study product creation.

Madam C.J. Walker (December 23, 1867 – May 25, 1919) was an American businesswoman, hair care entrepreneur, tycoon and philanthropist. She made her fortune by developing and marketing a hugely successful line of beauty and hair products for black women. The Guinness Book of Records cites Walker as the first female, black or white, self-accomplished millionaire.

She was born Sarah Breedlove in Delta, Louisiana, the first member of her family born free. Her parents were slaves. At age 14, she married a man named Moses McWilliams and was widowed at age 20. She then moved to St. Louis, Missouri to join her brothers. Sarah worked as a laundress for as little as a dollar and a half a day, but she was able to save enough to educate her daughter. While living in St. Louis, she joined the St. Paul's African Methodist Episcopal Church, who helped develop her speaking, interpersonal and organizational skills. She was married in 1894 to John Davis, and divorced about nine years later.

Her idea for a line of hair care products came to her when she began to lose her hair. Like many other Americans in the early 1900s, Walker's home lacked indoor plumbing, electricity and central heating. And like many women of that era, she washed her hair only once a month. As a result, she suffered from severe dandruff and scalp disease that caused her to go nearly bald. In 1905, Sarah moved to Denver, Colorado, working as a sales agent for Annie Malone, another black woman entrepreneur who manufactured hair care products. She also consulted with a Denver pharmacist, who analyzed Malone's formula and helped Walker formulate her own products. In addition, she often told reporters that the ingredients for her "Wonderful Hair Grower" had come to her in a dream.

Product Creation: Registering Your Domain Name
It's important to brand your company and use your company name as your domain name. Check to see if it's available and register a domain name. You can register any available domain name at GoDaddy.com, Mydomain.com, or Register.com

Kristen's Thoughts of the Day:
Madam C. J. Walker was an American businesswoman, hair care entrepreneur, tycoon and philanthropist. She is the first person to be a self-accomplished millionaire. It's in the Guinness Book of Records too. How cool is that!

Daddy's Thoughts of the Day:
Here is an awesome story about hard work and its reward. She is the first black woman millionaire in the late 1800's! Wow. You can't get a better example than that. The thing about it is you or anybody can do what she has done; with the right

principles, guts, and determination, one could conquer much! Creative hard work for yourself, (not your boss!) can make you prosperous. Think of something you can do to enrich your life as a whole and don't settle for a regular nine-to-five, only to retire broke and unhappy. That is not the road we as a family will travel.

Which Hosting Service Will You Use
Sunday April 27, 2008

Daily Meditation: Morning and Evening (6:00-6:10am) and (4:30-4:40pm)
Ecclesiastes 2:21
For a man may do his work with wisdom, knowledge and skill, and then he must leave all he owns to someone who has not worked for it. This too is meaningless and a great misfortune.

SOULFUL SUNDAY

We should look to overflow our spirits with something good. A good word produces a good feeling. Today, we should remain in the place of peace, filling our soul with the joy and happiness from the word. Surround yourself with people of like faith and celebrate life. Remember to enjoy life on this day. Synagogue, temple, mosque, or church, whatever your faith we should be humane to one another. Seek to fill yourself with an empowering word that will keep you motivated and inspired with the love you see all around us.

"I don't know the key to success, but the key to failure is trying to please everybody."
 --Bill Cosby

Definition Word: Optimistic
2. An inclination to put the most favorable construction upon actions and events or to anticipate the best possible outcome

5:00 – 6:00
Book Study:

Bill Cosby

6:30 – 7:00pm
Writing Section: In this section we will study and learn about Bill Cosby for thirty minutes, define the words we don't know or understand, and study product creation.

Bill Cosby (born William Henry Cosby, Jr. on July 12, 1937) is an American comedian, actor, television producer, and activist. A veteran stand-up performer, he got his start at various clubs, and then landed a vanguard role in the 1960s action show "I Spy". He later starred in his own series, "The Bill Cosby Show", in the late 1980s. He was one of the major characters on the children's television show "The Electric Company" for its first two seasons, and created the humorous educational cartoon series "Fat Albert" and the "Cosby Kids", about a group of young friends growing up in the city. Cosby also acted in numerous films.

During the 1980s, Cosby produced and starred in what is considered one of the decade's defining sitcoms, "The Cosby Show", which lasted eight seasons from 1984 to 1992, and is still in syndication. The sitcom highlighted the experiences and growth of an upper middle-class African-American family.

In the 1990s, Cosby starred in "Cosby", which first aired in 1996, hosted "Kids Say the Darndest Things", which began in 1998, and appeared in a number of movies. He has also appeared on the stand-up circuit.

Product Creation: Which Hosting Service Will You Use

After you have registered a name you now need somewhere to place or house your newly created domain name. These are called Hosting Services. You want to research your hosting provider to make sure that you are set up with an ecommerce account and not a personal account. You would need e-mail aliases, protection of customer data, security systems, and server space.

A great place to get started is with the company that currently provides you with your email services. Network Solutions, Affinity Internet, Intuit, and Yahoo offer a great small business hosting package designed especially for small businesses.

Kristen's Thoughts of the Day:
He is an American comedian, actor, television producer, and activist. I think Bill Cosby is a funny person. I liked his old show "The Cosby Show".

Daddy's Thoughts of the Day:
It is said that we should labor with wisdom, knowledge, and skill. As you develop your skills, writing skill, people skills, learning skills, you will develop the knowledge and wisdom in time. Right now, at your age of eleven, you will grow to be awesome in the future. Keep doing what you're doing and stay focused. One day you will awake being this great person.

Attitude and personality can take you a long way. The power to make a person laugh or smile is a lasting impression. Always be yourself and never force or try too hard to make people laugh. Let it be natural. Just know that whatever happens in life, you are free from any type of psychological or mental bondage. Free your mind and clear any negative feelings. Erase any negative learned behaviors that you can recognize. Pray daily and keep a positive outlook on life at all times.

Day 20:
Building Your Website
Monday April 28, 2008

Daily Meditation: Morning and Evening (6:00-6:10am) and (4:30-4:40pm)
Matthew 7:7-8
"Ask and it will be given to you; seek and you will find; knock and the door will be opened to you. 8. For everyone who asks receives, and who seeks finds; and to him who knocks, the door will be opened."

MINDFUL MONDAY

As we return back to our regular schedule, keep in mind our experiences and the mistakes we have made. Create new opportunities and new approaches to situations we don't understand. Relax and think calmly on things that puzzle us. Ask for clarity and look for the answer. Seek always to make better choices than before. Be aware of what we think, do, and speak so that we can live a life that keeps us in the place of peace.

I'd like to state that Spike Lee is not saying that African American culture is just for black people alone to enjoy and cherish. Culture is for everybody.
--Spike Lee

Definition Word: Attitude
4 a: a mental position with regard to a fact or state b: a feeling or emotion toward a fact or state 6: an organismic state of readiness to respond in a characteristic way to a stimulus (as an object, concept, or situation) 7 a: a negative or hostile state of mind b: a cool, cocky, defiant, or arrogant manner

5:00 – 6:00
Book Study:
Spike Lee

6:30 – 7:00pm
Writing Section: In this section we will study and learn about Spike Lee for thirty minutes. Define the words we don't know or understand. And study product creation for thirty minutes.

Shelton Jackson Lee (born March 20, 1957, in Atlanta, Georgia), better known as Spike Lee, is an Emmy Award-winning, and Academy Award-nominated American film director, producer, writer, and actor noted for his films dealing with controversial social and political issues. He also teaches film at New York University and Columbia University. His production company, 40 Acres & A Mule Filmworks, has produced over 35 films since 1983.

Lee was born in Atlanta, Georgia to Bill Lee and Jacquelyn Shelton Lee. Lee moved with his family to Brooklyn, New York when he was a small child. The Fort Greene neighborhood is home of Lee's production company, 40 Acres & A Mule Filmworks, and other Lee-owned or related businesses. As a child, his mother nicknamed him "Spike." In Brooklyn, he attended John Dewey High School. Lee enrolled in Morehouse College where he made his first student film, Last Hustle in Brooklyn. He took film courses at Clark Atlanta University and graduated with a B.A. in Mass Communication from Morehouse College. He then enrolled in New York University's Tisch School of the Arts. He graduated in 1978 with a Master of Fine Arts in Film & Television.

Product Creation: Building Your Website

Now it's time to build your own website. Websites can be very costly if you outsource another company to do the job. They are good at what they do and you will have a professional looking page, however, I recommend if you're just starting out to take advantage of the free services that are out there for site building. Here is a company that will give you a free webpage and hosting for $10 a month per domain you register. I joined because of their affiliate program to use as another source of income. The goal is to create another cash flow. The money you make from affiliate programs you would use to create more products and continue growth. This is how all the internet marketing millionaires got started and made their money. My websites are,

www.Kingicdc.com
www.Jonestownpublishing.com
www.mjproconsultants.com

Affiliate programs are designed for people that are in the industry of network marketing or have just start investing in the business of e-commerce. Thinking about starting your own online business then affiliate programs are for you to get a boost and a little help from your service provider. Almost every thing you would need to get started in e-commerce has an affiliate program. It would greatly benefit you to recommend someone to the same service you are using. For instance, the web page I'm using is the same company I use to promote my books and other online businesses. Why not recommend people to this service to get some money back each month? All I would ask is that you use those links that I have provided for you so that you can go under my identification.

Every service provider has a policy that states if you send them a customer they would reward you for your recommendations. They appreciate your referrals. This affiliate program gives you a website to advertise on and to use as a page where you direct all of your traffic. You will see that this will come in handy when you are doing your marketing campaigns for your business.

Kristen's Thoughts of the Day:
Spike Lee is an Emmy Award -winning, and Academy Award -nominated American film director, producer, writer and actor. He graduated in 1978 with a Master of Fine Arts in Film & Television at the age of 21. I didn't know you could graduate so early.

Daddy's Thoughts of the Day:
We all are here on earth traveling fast through space and time. We can't leave just yet. Therefore we need to get along with all cultures and religions. Embrace them with love and open arms. Never hate but understand each other's misfortunes. You are only better due to the disciplined use of the principles you have learned. Read and reread your book until you have these concepts buried deep within your soul. You can pass these same thoughts and ideas that have carried you though life more abundantly down to your kids.

Day 21:
Your Shopping-Cart
Tuesday April 29, 2008

Daily Meditation: Morning and Evening (6:00-6:10am) and (4:30-4:40pm)
Jude 1:10
"Yet these men speak abusively against whatever they do not understand; and what things they do understand by instinct, like unreasoning animals-these are the very things that destroy them".

TRUSTFUL TUESDAY

Today choose faith over fear and make a conscious effort to be courageous and strong. As we trust in God, the choices we make, and the people in our lives believe that he will see us through to the next stage of our journey. We may not know what is going on at the present moment. Pray, meditate and just trust that God will take care of us. Have no doubts or fears about trusting in what God has planned for you regardless to if you can see his plans or not .Until his plans are revealed just trust.

"It Don't Mean a Thing If It Ain't Got That Swing"
--Duke Ellington

Definition Word: Desire
1: to long or hope for: exhibit or feel desire for (desire success) 2 a: to express a wish for: request barchaic: to express a wish to: ask

5:00 – 6:00
Book Study:
Duke Ellington

6:30 – 7:00pm
Writing Section: In this section we will study and learn about Duke Ellington for thirty minutes, define the words we don't know or understand, and study product creation.

Edward Kennedy "Duke" Ellington (April 29, 1899 – May 24, 1974) was an American composer, pianist, and bandleader, recognized during his life as one of the most influential figures in jazz, if not in all American music. Ellington's reputation has increased since his death, including a special award citation from the Pulitzer Prize Board.

Ellington called his style and sound "American Music" rather than jazz, and liked to describe those who impressed him as "beyond category", including many of the musicians who served with his orchestra, some of whom were themselves considered among the giants of jazz and remained with Ellington's orchestra for decades. While many were noteworthy in their own right, it was Ellington that melded them into one of the most well-known orchestral units in the history of jazz. He often composed specifically for the style and skills of these individuals, such as "Jeep's Blues" for Johnny Hodges, "Concerto for Cootie" ("Do Nothing Till You Hear from Me") for Cootie Williams and "The Mooche" for Tricky Sam Nanton. He also recorded songs written by his bandsmen, such as Juan Tizol's "Caravan" and "Perdido" which brought the "Spanish Tinge" to big-band jazz. After 1941, he frequently collaborated with composer-arranger Billy Strayhorn, whom he called his alter-ego.

One of the twentieth century's best-known African-American celebrities, Ellington recorded for many American record companies, and appeared in several films. Ellington and his orchestra toured the United States and Europe regularly before and after World War II. Ellington led his band from 1923 until his death in 1974. His son Mercer Ellington took over the band until his death from cancer in 1996. Paul Ellington, Mercer's youngest son, took over the Orchestra from there and after his mother's passing took over the estate of Duke and Mercer Ellington.

Product Creation: Your Shopping-cart
Your webpage will need a shopping-cart. The software makes it very easy for your customers to process orders online. These shopping-carts can determine shipping costs, calculate sales tax, and send electronic order confirmations. I would recommend you use GoEcart, IShoppingcart, and ShopSite, as these are some of the better ones.

Kristen's Thoughts of the Day:
He was an American composer, pianist and bandleader. He called his style and sound "American music" instead of jazz. He was one of the twentieth century's best-known African-American celebrities.

Daddy's Thoughts of the Day:
In our business program we take them through and mentor them in starting and operating their own business. We have an expert team of business leaders and

entrepreneurs. This would enable applicants to learn his/her business at an early age. We will take them by the hand and run their business for them so that they can learn the proper way of doing business. After they have proven they can operate their business on their own, only then, will we turn it over to them. Even then, if they need our help, we will be there for them.

Each applicant would have a set of goals put forth for them to accomplish. It can be anything from starting a business, machining designs, inventing, robotics and computer science, basically anything productive and creative to enough to provide information on various economic growth. Young people need trades and ways of making money. By teaching them to start businesses they will have products created and designed for that particular community demographic. We will teach them to start businesses like used car dealers and body shops, whereas King Industry's body Shops will train our community youth to paint and work in a body shop environment. The used car dealership business will show them how to buy auctioned cars, buy a lot for their cars, and sell their cars on their properties.

Then we would show another how to start a machine shop and this is where we would out source our mechanic work for our cars. Kids will have the option of learning it all or in steps; however it goes they can learn.

- Publishing Company- Jonestown Publishing
- Dog Kennel- Mastiff Express
- Real Estate Company- M & J Property Consultants
- Beauty Suppy-Kribre Beauty Supplies
- Etc......

These businesses alone would raise 65% of King Industry's capital. One quest and purpose we don't want to forget is the quest for knowledge and unity among people. Our nonprofit organizations, business structure is networking between multiple businesses owned by King Industries Members. One member would own the mechanic shop; another member would own the auto body shop, and the dealer shop. Therefore we can train the rest of the community to do the same thing. We will create a network of business leaders, from an early age within the same community.

Jude 1:10
"Yet these men speak abusively against whatever they do not understand; and what things they do understand by instinct, like unreasoning animals-these are the very things that destroy them".

Understand that you or not here to please anyone. And you're not going to make everyone happy. Be brave enough to be yourself and surround yourself with like minded people. You have religions fighting, countries, and people on the street dying trying to eat. Stand against poverty, injustices, and the bigotry of the world. The world is only going to get worse before it gets better. With that said don't waste time worrying about the "dumb stuff", in life. Do what you're supposed to do now, so that you can easily transition from one stage to another later on in life. As we grow our business I want you to grow with it. Sharpening your skills so that you can learn to produce more books, videos, designs, inventions, etc.... I want you to hold on to your desire, as we continue to learn and grow our businesses.

Day 22:
Site Promotion
Wednesday April 30, 2008

Daily Meditation: Morning and Evening (6:00-6:10am) and (4:30-4:40pm)
Revelation 1:7
"Look, he is coming with the clouds, and every eye will see him, even those who
pierced him; and all the people of the earth will mourn because of him. So shall it
be! Amen".

WONDERFUL WEDNESDAY

Throughout our day, we want to reflect on how blessed we are and how beautiful
life is. We want to do our best to honor ourselves and our spirit. We want to remain
humble throughout the day, never forgetting that God is not mocked. We want to
remember to work hard at accomplishing our goals and increasing our talents and
skills, stay focused on the task at hand so that we may excel in all that we do. Put
forth effort at being the best person we can be, knowing that we are whole,
together, generous, balanced, and well-rounded. We will not be afraid to let our
light shine through and make a difference in the lives of others. Regardless of what
the day may bring, we will remain in the position of Godliness.

There is nothing so disobedient as an undisciplined mind, and there is nothing so
obedient as a disciplined mind.
--Buddha

Definition Word: witty
1. Archaic: having good intellectual capacity: intelligent 2. amusingly or
ingeniously clever in conception or execution

5:00 – 6:00
Book Study:
Gautama Buddha

6:30 – 7:00pm
Writing Section: In this section we will study and learn about Gautama Buddha
for thirty minutes, define the words we don't know or understand, and study
product creation.

Siddhārtha Gautama, in Sanskrit, or Siddhattha Gotama, in Pali, was a spiritual teacher from ancient India and the founder of Buddhism. He is generally recognized by Buddhists as the Supreme Buddha (Sammāsambuddha) of our age. The precise nature of such a supreme Buddha - whether "merely" human or a transcendental, immortal, god-transcending being - is differently construed in Theravada and Mahayana Buddhism. Theravada tends to view him as a super-human personage of supreme teaching skill and wisdom (uncontestable after his physical death), whereas Mahayana Buddhism goes further and tends to see him as a projection of an eternal, ultimate principle of Buddhahood (see Dharmakaya), present in all phenomena, immortal and transcendent.[citation needed] The time of his birth and death are uncertain: most early 20th-century historians date his lifetime from circa 563 BCE to 483 BCE; more recently, however, at a specialist symposium on this question, the majority of those scholars who presented definite opinions gave dates within 20 years either side of 400 BCE for the Buddha's death, with others supporting earlier or later dates.

Product Creation: Site Promotion

In the promotion of your website, make sure to incorporate your offline marketing and advertising strategies. Include your URL on all advertisements and marketing materials. Microsoft gives a step-by-step format of a Website marketing campaign.

Kristen's Thoughts of the Day:
His life was so interesting!

Daddy's Thoughts of the Day:
I'm doing my best to raise this family in the word of God. And I know you don't understand everything right now but trust me in due time it will catch hold and the seeds planted inside you will grow.

I can't really tell you what that bible verse means. It seems simple and self explanatory but I'll let you talk to someone who is more gifted in that area than I. I'm not a preacher but we do have four in the family. I'll ask all four of them what it means. I think that all will know the power of His word. It doesn't matter who you are, white, black, yellow, brown, rich or poor. Apply it and give it time to grow and wake up one morning with the results. It can "kinda" sneak up on you, so be ready. It happens very fast, as well. Years of hard work will pay off. God will not be mocked!

Day 23:
Site Security
Thursday May 1, 2008

Daily Meditation: Morning and Evening (6:00-6:10am) and (4:30-4:40pm)
3 John 1:4
I have no greater joy than to hear that my children are walking in the truth.

THANKFUL THURSDAY

Today we want to give thanks, remembering all the things we should be thankful for. We should choose to be thankful for our experiences, good or bad, our friends, family, and most importantly our health. We should be thankful for who we are now and what we are to become. Our words of thanksgiving will be received through our prayers, our spirit, our actions and our songs. We will be still in our spirit, anxious for nothing, but thankful for all.

Education is the key to unlock the golden door of freedom.
--George Washington Carver

Definition Word: Nimrod- "A mighty hunter before the Lord."
"The first written account of Nimrod in the Bible is attributed to the Jewish according to the "documentary hypothesis."

5:00 – 6:00pm
Book Study:
George Washington Carver

6:30 – 7:00pm
Writing Section: In this section we will study and learn about George Washington Carver for thirty minutes, define the words we don't know or understand, and study product creation.

George Washington Carver (July 12, 1864 – January 5, 1943) worked in agricultural extension at the Tuskegee Institute, in Tuskegee, Alabama, teaching former slaves farming techniques for self-sufficiency. His exact birth day (and year) is unknown, yet it is known that it was some time before slavery was abolished in Missouri in January, 1865. To commemorate his life and fabulous inventions, George Washington Carver Recognition Day is celebrated every January 5, on the day Carver died.

To bring education to farmers, Carver designed a mobile school, called a Jesup Wagon after the New York financier, Morris Ketchum Jesup, who provided funding. In 1921, Carver spoke in favor of a peanut tariff before the Ways and Means Committee of the United States House of Representatives. At the time it was unusual for a black person to be called as an expert. Carver's well received testimony earned him national attention, and he became an unofficial spokesman for the peanut industry. Carver wrote 44 practical agricultural bulletins for farmers.

George Washington's father died in a fatal ox-hauling agricultural trip. One of the supply wagons toppled, thereby suffocating him.

In the Reconstruction South, an agricultural monoculture of cotton depleted the soil, and, in the early 20th century, the boll weevil destroyed much of the cotton crop. Much of Carver's fame was based on his research and promotion of alternative crops to cotton, such as peanuts and sweet potatoes. He wanted poor farmers to grow alternative crops as both a source of their own food as well as a source of other products to improve their quality of life. His most popular bulletin contained 105 existing food recipes that used peanuts. He also created or disseminated about 100 products made from peanuts that were useful for the house and farm, including cosmetics, dyes, paints, plastics, gasoline, and nitroglycerin.

Product Creation: Site Security
You need to develop a privacy policy and secure your site. This is to ensure your customers that their online data is protected; now, customers can feel like they can trust you. For developing privacy and security policies, The eCom Resource Center has guidelines for developing these privacy and security policies. The technology that protects your customers by encrypting and authenticating it is Secure Socket Layer (SSL). You can get your SSL from VeriSign, Comodo, and GoDaddy.

Kristen's Thoughts of the Day:
I think that Carver was a hard working person. He worked in agricultural extension at the Tuskegee Institute, in Tuskegee, Alabama, teaching former slaves farming techniques for self-sufficiency. He was so smart.

Daddy's Thoughts of the Day:
For a long time I thought that the word "Nimrod" meant "stupid"; now I found out that it is because of Bugs Bunny I thought that. Bugs Bunny called Elmer Fudd a Nimrod because he was a corky hunter. Bugs Bunny was being sarcastic. I've

heard it in songs and used by many people and it always sounded negative to me. I looked it up one day and come to find out that it meant "mighty hunter before the lord." I was shocked and the lesson I learned was to do my own research and gain the information myself. Don't just listen to everything you hear. "Prove all things" it says somewhere in the bible. And that lesson stays with me still to this day. You're not being snotty or trying to be a know-it-all. You want to be confident of your words being true. To be a lady of Powerful Words, you have to be sure your words are accurate.

Day 24:
Your Customer Service Policies and Procedures
Friday May 2, 2008

Daily Meditation: Morning and Evening (6:00-6:10am) and (4:30-4:40pm)
Proverbs 27:19
As in water face reflects face, so the heart of man reflects man.

FAITHFUL FRIDAY

Its important that we awaken to all that we are meant to be through our journey in life. Our faithfulness to ourselves will allow us to be patient in life as we become more of who we are meant to be. We should be faithful to longsuffering, bearing of pain, and dealing with trials without complaint. We should be faithful in showing self-control with others, as well as ourselves. Our faith will cause us to fight against any adversity, cause us to be focused, and fearless. Have faith throughout this day.

A life is not important except in the impact it has on other lives.
--Jackie Robinson

Definition Word: Conscience
It's a hypothesized ability or faculty that distinguishes whether our actions are right or wrong. It leads to feelings of remorse when we do things that go against our moral values and to feelings of rectitude or integrity when our actions conform to our moral values.

5:00 – 6:00
Book Study:

Jackie Robinson

6:30 – 7:00pm
Writing Section: In this section we will study and learn about Jackie Robinson for thirty minutes, define the words we don't know or understand, and study product creation.

Jack Roosevelt "Jackie" Robinson (January 31, 1919 – October 24, 1972) became the first African-American Major League baseball player of the modern era in 1947. While not the first African American professional baseball player in United States history, his Major League debut with the Brooklyn Dodgers ended approximately eighty years of baseball segregation, also known as the baseball color line, or color barrier. In the United States at this time, many white people believed that blacks and whites should be segregated or kept apart in many phases of life, including sports and daily life.

The Baseball Hall of Fame inducted Robinson in 1962 and he was a member of six World Series teams. He earned six consecutive All-Star Game nominations and won several awards during his career. In 1947, Robinson won The Sporting News Rookie of the Year Award and the first Rookie of the Year Award. Two years later, he was awarded the National League MVP Award. In addition to his accomplishments on the field, Jackie Robinson was also a forerunner of the Civil Rights Movement. In the 1960s, he was a key figure in the establishment and growth of the Freedom National Bank, an African-American owned and controlled entity based in Harlem, New York. He also wrote a syndicated newspaper column for a number of years, in which he was an outspoken supporter of Martin Luther King Jr. and Malcolm X.

Robinson engaged in political campaigning for a number of politicians, including the Democrat Hubert Humphrey and the Republican Richard Nixon. In recognition of his accomplishments, Robinson was posthumously awarded a Congressional Gold Medal and the Presidential Medal of Freedom.

On April 15, 1997, the 50 year anniversary of his debut, Major League Baseball retired the number 42, the number Robinson wore, in recognition of his accomplishments both on and off the field in a ceremony at Shea Stadium. In 1950, he was the subject of a film biography, The Jackie Robinson Story, in which he played himself. He became a political activist in his post-playing days.

In 1946, Robinson married Rachel Annetta Isum. In 1973, after Jackie died, Rachel founded the Jackie Robinson Foundation.

Product Creation: Your Customer Service Policies and Procedures

If you have an existing business, mirror the level of services you provide by developing customer service policies. You will need policies stating product returns. Will they return it to a local store or mail it back to the company? Look at your customer service options. You can decide on a web-based customer service through 24/7 chat, e-mail, and of course the use of a toll-free telephone customer service support. www.WorkZ.com has a comprehensive detailed plan for developing an online customer service plan.

Kristen's Thoughts of the Day:

If he was still alive he would be the best baseball player in the world. Well, that's my opinion.

Daddy's Thoughts of the Day:

Be aware of generational bondage and how it affects people and their lives through the poor belief patterns that they live by and pass down to their kids. The programmed behavior patterns of people will keep them in a state of poverty. If it is learned, then it can be unlearned. People get to the point where they can't live for themselves, they can't think for themselves. History shows that if you can't think for yourself, then someone will think for you. If you don't know your place in life, someone will put you in a place.

Not cool, have control over your thoughts and life. I know poverty is not the poor man's dream! Be the person that is doing the thinking and not the person being told what to do and how to do it, unable to think for yourself. Use your words to heal others. Be a loving, and fearless, light, shining bright for the enlightenment of humanity type of person.

Day 25:
Accepting Payment
Saturday May 3, 2008

Daily Meditation: Morning and Evening (6:00-6:10am) and (4:30-4:40pm)
Philemon 1:16
No longer as a slave, but better than a slave, as a dear brother. He is very dear to me but even dearer to you, both as a man and as a brother in the Lord.

SUCCESSFUL SATURDAY

To have made it to Successful Saturday is truly a wonderful success. Throughout the week we have walked by faith, renewed our minds and spirit, and have trusted in the all-powerful universe. We have maintained a wonderful character and we are thankful for whom we are and all that we have. To remain strong and in character throughout the week is truly defined as a success.

A man is but the product of his thoughts what he thinks, he becomes.
--Mahatma Gandhi

Definition Word: Character
2 a: one of the attributes or features that make up and distinguish an individual

5:00 – 6:00
Book Study:
Mahatma Gandhi

6:30 – 7:00pm
Writing Section: In this section we will study and learn about and Mahatma Gandhi for thirty minutes, define the words we don't know or understand, and study product creation.

Mahatma Karamchand Gandhi (October 2, 1869 – January 30, 1948) was a major political and spiritual leader of India and the Indian independence movement. He was the pioneer of Satyagraha—resistance to tyranny through mass civil disobedience, firmly founded upon ahimsa or total non-violence—which led India to independence and inspired movements for civil rights and freedom across the world. He is commonly known in India and across the world as Mahatma Gandhi or "Great Soul", (an epithet given by Rabindranath Tagore) and as Bapu (Gujarati: or "Father"). In India, he is officially accorded the honour of Father of the Nation.

2 October, his birthday, is commemorated each year as Gandhi Jayanti, a national holiday. On 15 June 2007, the United Nations General Assembly unanimously adopted a resolution declaring 2 October to be the "International Day of Non-Violence".

Product Creation: Accepting Payment

We want to offer our customers convenient ways of making payments to our company. You will need to accept payments and track your online sales. Therefore, you will need to set up an online merchant account. If you have a business bank account, ask your banker about connecting your online merchant account to your existing merchant account. You then can accept online credit card payments. Set up your gateway account to process your orders. You can do this by going to: Authorize.Net and CyberSource. And of course, PayPal offers a free service for processing online payments.

Kristen's Thoughts of the Day:
Mahatma Gandhi was the leader of India. He was the major political and spiritual leader of the Indian independence movement. He was considered the Father of the Indian Nation.

Daddy's Thoughts of the Day:
Have control over your thoughts. Program your thoughts for success. How do you program your thoughts? The same way you learned your ABC's when I taught them to you a long time ago. You have to use the repetition method. Like singing a song, it sticks like that. We meditate on the word daily, singing praise to the Lord. And we use the techniques of our Rites of Passage Program to get it inside of us. Knowledge to live by!

A man is but the product of his thoughts what he thinks, he becomes.
--Mahatma Gandhi

A great person like Mahatma Gandhi believed that his thoughts were powerful, and they created and shaped everything in his environment. We study various people so that we can learn of some of the amazing characters of people captured and consumed by history. I share this because I find it valuable, and it means a lot to me to read and experience this with my family.

Daily Meditation: Morning and Evening (6:00-6:10am) and (4:30-4:40pm)
3 John 1:2
Dear friend, I pray that you may enjoy good health and that all may go well with you, even as your soul is getting along well.

SOULFUL SUNDAY

We should look to overflow our spirits with something good. A good word produces a good feeling. Today, we should remain in the place of peace, filling our soul with the joy and happiness from the Word. Surround yourself with people of like faith and celebrate life. Remember to enjoy life on this day. Synagogue, temple, mosque, or church, whatever your faith we should be humane to one another. Seek to fill yourself with an empowering word that will keep you motivated and inspired with the love you see all around us.

You're not to be so blind with patriotism that you can't face reality. Wrong is wrong, no matter who does it or says it.
--Malcolm X

Definition Word: Balance
1. Stability of mind or body:

5:00 – 6:00
Book Study:

Malcolm -X

6:30 – 7:00pm
Writing Section: In this section we will study and learn about and Malcolm-X for thirty minutes, define the words we don't know or understand, and study product creation.

Malcolm X (born Malcolm Little; May 19, 1925 – February 21, 1965), also known as El-Hajj Malik El-Shabazz, was an American Black Muslim minister and a spokesman for the Nation of Islam.

After leaving the Nation of Islam in 1964, he made the pilgrimage, the Hajj, to Mecca and became a Muslim. He also founded the Muslim Mosque, Inc. and the Organization of Afro-American Unity. Less than a year later, he was assassinated in Washington Heights on the first day of National Brotherhood Week.

Historian Robin D.G. Kelley wrote, "Malcolm X has been called many things: Pan-Africanist, father of Black Power, religious fanatic, closet conservative, incipient socialist, and a menace to society. The meaning of his public life — his politics and ideology — is contested in part because his entire body of work consists of a few dozen speeches and a collaborative autobiography whose veracity is challenged. Malcolm has become a sort of tabula rasa, or blank slate, on which people of different positions can write their own interpretations of his politics and legacy. Chuck D of the rap group Public Enemy and Supreme Court Justice Clarence Thomas can both declare Malcolm X their hero."

Product Creation: Filling Your Orders

When your orders start to come in, you should have already decided on who was going to process your orders. Will you hire someone, do it yourself, or use a third party, (spouse or family member)? Look into how you will package your order. USPS has a good bulk service for publishers where they give you discounts for bulk orders with a bulk drop off box. So, make sure that you have everything in order for processing and delivery before hand.

Kristen's Thoughts of the Day:
During the book study we learned what stability means. I didn't at first know what it meant. Then I looked it up and then we continued our study.
Stability - the quality or attribute of being firm and steadfast

Daddy's Thoughts of the Day:
We all are human and sometimes we sin! However, I want you to stand strong in your conviction of the family morals and values you learned. Do not be afraid to stand up for righteousness! For the King Sits on the Throne of Righteousness. Understand your enemies so that you will know how to combat them. And do it with the power of your words, MY Little Lady!

Daily Meditation: Morning and Evening (6:00-6:10am) and (4:30-4:40pm)
Psalm 1:1
Blessed is the man who does not walk in the counsel of the wicked or stand in the way of sinners or sit in the seat of mockers.

MINDFULL MONDAY

As we return back to our regular schedule, keep in mind our experiences and the mistakes we have made. Create new opportunities and new approaches to situations we don't understand. Relax and think calmly on things that puzzle us. Ask for clarity and look for the answer. Seek always to make better choices than before. Be aware of what we think, do, and speak so that we can live a life that keeps us in the place of peace.

It is time for parents to teach young people early on that in diversity there is beauty and there is strength. We all should know that diversity makes for a rich tapestry, and we must understand that all the threads of that tapestry are equal in value no matter their color.
--Maya Angelou

Definition Word: Skills
2 a: the ability to use one's knowledge effectively and readily in execution or performance b: dexterity or coordination especially in the execution of learned physical tasks 3: a learned power of doing something competently: a developed aptitude or ability

5:00 – 6:00
Book Study:

Maya Angelou

6:30 – 7:00pm
Writing Section: In this section we will study and learn about and Maya Angelou for thirty minutes, define the words we don't know or understand, and study product creation.

Maya Angelou, (born Marguerite Ann Johnson, April 4, 1928) is an American poet, memoirist, actress and an important figure in the American Civil Rights Movement. Angelou is known for her series of six autobiographies, starting with, <u>I Know Why the Caged Bird Sings</u>, (1969) which was nominated for a National Book Award and called her magnum opus. Her volume of poetry, just Give Me a Cool Drink of Water 'Fore I Diiie (1971) was nominated for the Pulitzer Prize.

Angelou recited her poem, <u>On the Pulse of Morning</u> at President Bill Clinton's inauguration in 1993. She has been highly honored for her body of work, including being awarded over 30 honorary degrees.

Product Creation: Search Engine Optimization (SEO)

As a new online business you want to rank as high as possible in the search engines. Connected to the homepage of your website you will have to enter key words about your business and product. Use words that will attract the attention of your audience. It's good practice to look at your competitors to see how they target the market.

You would want to use heading tags and subheading tags to include key words. In the page title syntax area describe what you do. You would put this in the description portion of your website before the company name.

Next, you should get your business listed in directories. There are some that are free, like <u>DMOZ.com</u> and others. However, Yahoo will charge an annul fee of $299. I hear it is very much worth it. Give free articles to social networks and online forums, as this will further get your business name out there. Start a blog and an online forum so that customers can chat about your products and services. Also, get and setup analytical software to track your conversion rates. After making changes to your site, you want to see the conversion rates go up or down. This will give you a better understand as to what works and what dosen't.

Kristen's Thoughts of the Day:
My mom talks about Maya Angelou all the time and thinks that her work is very good. She is known for her book, <u>I Know Why the Caged Birds Sings</u>.

Daddy's Thoughts of the Day:
For this hour, we talked about Maya Angelou and the wonderful work she has done. We respect her and someday I want you to walk in dignity like her. We studied the meaning of "skill", our definition word of the day, and why it is

important to acquire different skills. I will repeat the same important information over and over again until it sticks. Definitions, reading, writing and prayer are the tools and resources we use to excel. Education is very important and you must learn to overcome the hardships of the world.

Daily Meditation: Morning and Evening (6:00-6:10am) and (4:30-4:40pm)
Daniel 4:27
Therefore, O king, be pleased to accept my advice: Renounce your sins by doing what is right, and your wickedness by being kind to the oppressed. It may be that then your prosperity will continue."

TRUSTFUL TUESDAY

Today, choose faith over fear and make a conscious effort to be courageous and strong. As we trust in God, the choices we make, and the people in our lives believe that he will see us through to the next stage of our journey. We may not know what is going on at the present moment. Pray, meditate and just trust that God will take care of us. Have no doubts or fears about trusting in what God has planned for you regardless to if you can see his plans or not .Until his plans are revealed just trust.

Every great dream begins with a dreamer. Always remember, you have within you the strength, the patience, and the passion to reach for the stars to change the world.
--Harriet Tubman

Definition Word: Rites of Passage
Is a ritual that marks a change in a person's social or physical status. Rites of passage are often ceremonies surrounding events such as childbirth, menarche or other milestones within puberty, coming of age, marriage, weddings, and death. Initiation ceremonies such as baptism, confirmation and bar or bat mitzvahs are considered important rites of passage. In the last centuries, Western society has seen a steady decline in the use of and potential benefits rising from male rites of passage.

5:00 – 6:00
Book Study:

Harriet Tubman

6:30 – 7:00pm
Writing Section: In this section we will study and learn about and Harriet Tubman for thirty minutes, define the words we don't know or understand, and study product creation.

Harriet Tubman (born Araminta Ross, c. 1820 – 10 March 1913) was an African-American abolitionist, humanitarian, and Union spy during the U.S. Civil War. After escaping from captivity, she made thirteen missions to rescue over seventy slaves using the network of antislavery activists and safe houses known as the Underground Railroad. She later helped John Brown recruit men for his raid on Harpers Ferry, and in the post-war era struggled for women's suffrage.

Born into slavery in Dorchester County, Maryland, Tubman was beaten and whipped by her various owners as a child. Early in her life, she suffered a traumatic head wound when an irate slave owner threw a heavy metal weight at her, intending to hit another slave. The injury caused disabling seizures, headaches, powerful visionary and dream activity, and spells of hypersomnia which occurred throughout her entire life. A devout Christian, she ascribed her visions and vivid dreams to premonitions from God.

In 1849, Tubman escaped to Philadelphia, then immediately returned to Maryland to rescue her family. Slowly, one group at a time, she brought relatives with her out of the state, and eventually guided dozens of other slaves to freedom. Traveling by night and in extreme secrecy, Tubman (or "Moses", as she was called) "never lost a passenger". Heavy rewards were offered for many of the people she helped bring away, but no one ever knew it was Harriet Tubman who was helping them. When a far-reaching United States Fugitive Slave Law was passed in 1850, she helped guide fugitives further north into Canada, and helped newly-freed slaves find work.

When the American Civil War began, Tubman worked for the Union Army, first as a cook and nurse, and then as an army scout and spy. The first woman to lead an armed expedition in the war, she guided the raid on the Combahee River, which liberated more than seven hundred slaves. After the war, she retired to the family home in Auburn, New York, where she cared for her aging parents. She was active in the women's suffrage movement until illness overtook her and she had to be admitted to a home for elderly African-Americans she had helped open years earlier. After she died in 1913, she became an icon of American courage and freedom.

Product Creation: Developing a Marketing Strategy

Share unique selling differentials and positions about your company. Explain what sets your business apart from your competition. Clearly describe your company's target audience. You should have information about your customers, the type of person that will take advantage of your products. A complete demographic will give information about your customer such as age, gender, income, location, education, and much more.

You should create a marketing budget. Become aware of ways to position your self in the marketplace. Define what market would best fit your product and marketing needs. This would include your advertisements, direct mailings, internet marketing and public relations, as well as other promotional means.

Kristen's Thoughts of the Day:
I think that Harriet Tubman is a kind of person that never gives up. That's pretty cool to me.

Daddy's Thoughts of the Day:
The Underground Railroad was like their rites of passage to freedom. We all should go through some sort of rites of passage to commiserate us into humanity. As the world grows and changes, it will continue to do so. It's not going to stop that process of nature. In the next fifty years, much will be different according to the speed of technology change. We must not get blinded by the times and left behind, but must stay up with the times and continue to hold on to what is most important to us in our lives. That is one thing that will never change, "The Power of Spoken Word".

Day 29:
Write a Business Plan
Wednesday May 7, 2008

Daily Meditation: Morning and Evening (6:00-6:10am) and (4:30-4:40pm)
Jeremiah 29:7
Also, seek the peace and prosperity of the city to which I have carried you into exile. Pray to the Lord for it, because if it prospers, you too will prosper."

WONDERFUL WEDNESDAY

Throughout our day, we want to reflect on how blessed we are and how beautiful life is. We want to do our best to honor ourselves and our spirit. We want to remain humble throughout the day, never forgetting that God is not mocked. We want to remember to work hard at accomplishing our goals and increasing our talents and skills, stay focused on the task at hand so that we may excel in all that we do. Put forth effort at being the best person we can be, knowing that we are whole, together, generous, balanced, and well-rounded. We will not be afraid to let our light shine through and make a difference in the lives of others. Regardless of what the day may bring, we will remain in the position of Godliness.

Challenges make you discover things about yourself that you never really knew. They're what make the instrument stretch-what make you go beyond the norm.
--Cicely Tyson

Definition Word: Ignorance- 1. The condition or quality of being ignorant; lack of knowledge, education, etc. 2.unawareness (*of*)

5:00 – 6:00
Book Study:

Cicely Tyson

102

6:30 – 7:00pm
Writing Section: In this section we will study and learn about and Cicely Tyson for thirty minutes, define the words we don't know or understand, and study product creation.

Tyson's parents, Theodosia and William Tyson, came from the islands of Nevis of Saint Kitts and Nevis in the West Indies, but she was born and raised in Harlem, New York City. Tyson was first discovered by a photographer for <u>Ebony</u> magazine, and became a popular fashion model. Her first film was an uncredited role in "Carib Gold" in 1957, but she went on to do television - the celebrated series East Side/West Side and the long-running soap opera "The Guiding Light".

In 1961, Tyson appeared in the original cast of French playwright Jean Genet's "The Blacks", the longest running Off-Broadway non-musical of the decade, running for 1,408 performances. The original cast also featured James Earl Jones, Roscoe Lee Browne, Louis Gossett, Jr., Godfrey Cambridge, Maya Angelou and Charles Gordone. Tyson starred opposite Sammy Davis Jr. in the film, "A Man Called Adam" (1966), starred in the film version of Graham Greene's "The Comedians" (1967), and had a featured role in "The Heart Is a Lonely Hunter" (1968).

In 1972, she was nominated for the Academy Award for Best Actress for her role in the critically acclaimed "Sounder". In 1974, she won two Emmy Awards for "The Autobiography of Miss Jane Pittman". Other acclaimed television roles included "Roots", "King", in which she portrayed Coretta Scott King, "The Marva Collins Story", "When No One Would Listen" and "Oldest Living Confederate Widow Tells All", for which she received her third Emmy award.

In 2005, Tyson co-starred in the movies "Because of Winn-Dixie" and "Diary of a Mad Black Woman". Also, the same year she was honored by Oprah Winfrey at her Legends Ball. She married famous jazz trumpeter Miles Davis on 26 November 1981 -- the ceremony was conducted by Atlanta mayor Andrew Young at the home of actor Bill Cosby. Tyson and Davis divorced in 1988. The Cicely Tyson school of Performing and Fine Arts, a magnet school in East Orange, New Jersey was renamed in her honor.

Product Creation: Write a Business Plan
This is a very important step for any business, large or small. If at anytime you would want to receive a loan or money from an investor, a business plan is what they would want to review. It's also a way of helping you, the owner, follow

through as planned. You would write your goals in your business plan to follow. Remember; be as realistic as possible when writing your business plan. There are many great business plan writers and software online to help you. You can use business.com to get you started in the right direction in writing your business plan.

Kristen's Thoughts of the Day:
At first I thought she was related to Mike Tyson, but she's not. I must have been sleepy that day.

Daddy's Thoughts of the Day:
The challenge of this Rites of passage program is to expand their minds. We will return next year with another forty day Rites of Passage Program. Both of my daughters will continue to grow and have fun doing it. I think that education should be fun and learning should be fun. Since pre-school, we put in their heads that learning and school was fun. I do that with college also. I tell them that college will be some of the best times of their lives. I show them college films. I read about successful people that have gone to college. I try to make it normal to do so and taboo not to go to college.

Day 30:
Building Your Brand
Thursday May 8, 2008

Daily Meditation: Morning and Evening (6:00-6:10am) and (4:30-4:40pm)
Deuteronomy 30:15
See, I set before you today life and prosperity, death and destruction.

THANKFUL THURSDAY

Today we want to give thanks, remembering all the things we should be thankful for. We should choose to be thankful for our experiences, good or bad, our friends, family, and most importantly our health. We should be thankful for who we are now and what we are to become. Our words of thanksgiving will be received through our prayers, our spirit, our actions and our songs. We will be still in our spirit, anxious for nothing, but thankful for all.

Definition Word: Humanity
1. The quality or state of being humane
2. The quality or state of being human

5:00 – 6:00
Book Study:

Earl G. Graves Jr.

6:30 – 7:00pm
Writing Section: In this section we will study and learn about and Earl G. Graves Jr. for thirty minutes define the words we don't know or understand, and study product creation.

Earl Gilbert "Butch" Graves, Jr. (born January 5, 1962, in Brooklyn, New York, US) is an African-American businessman and retired basketball player. He attended Scarsdale High School.

Graves, the son of Black Enterprise founder Earl G. Graves, Sr., attended Yale University and earned an MBA from Harvard University. While at Yale, he was a member of Skull and Bones and captained the college basketball team. He is currently the all-time leading scorer in Yale men's basketball history and third all-time in Ivy League. He was drafted into the NBA by the Philadelphia 76ers and later played briefly for the Cleveland Cavaliers (1984-85).

Graves has worked for Morgan Stanley, as president and CEO of Earl G. Graves Publishing Company, publisher of Black Enterprise, and director of Autozone, Inc.

In 1995, Graves was detained and searched by two New York Metro-North Police looking for a suspect who did not resemble Graves in any way except race. The police department publicly apologized and Metro-North Railroad purchased ads featuring a printed apology in three New York newspapers, including The New York Times.

Product Creation: Building Your Brand

You should find a stylish and unique way to create a good marketing idea that will separate you from the rest. Incorporate that same idea into your business plan for the purpose of staying fresh every time you look at your plan. Submit your plan to investors on your investors list so that they can start to ingest and get a feel for your branding ideas. As your brand develops, you should plaster your brand throughout your ecommerce avenues, bringing your company to the next stage of profitability.

Kristen's Thoughts of the Day:

His father is the founder of Black Enterprise and he is a retired basketball player. I wonder if he was as good as Magic Johnson. Well, I don't know.

Daddy's Thoughts of the Day:

What does being human mean to you? We all have choices in life where we must choose whether to be successful or not. Your choice can either hinder you or help you get where you need to be in life. It's no one's choice but your own. Don't place blame on anyone but yourself for the way your life turns out. Take life seriously now and know that there is a time and place for everything. There is a time to play and a time to work. If you work hard now, you can play even harder later!

Day 31:
You Are Your Business
Friday May 9, 2008

Daily Meditation: Morning and Evening (6:00-6:10am) and (4:30-4:40pm)
2 Corinthians 4:8-9
We are hard pressed on every side, but not crushed; perplexed, but not in despair, persecuted, but not abandoned; struck down, but not destroyed.

FAITHFUL FRIDAY

Its important that we awaken to all that we are meant to be through our journey in life. Our faithfulness to ourselves will allow us to be patient in life as we become more of who we are meant to be. We should be faithful to longsuffering, bearing of pain, and dealing with trials without complaint. We should be faithful in showing self-control with others, as well as ourselves. Our faith will cause us to fight against any adversity, cause us to be focused, and fearless. Have faith throughout this day.

I'm a lover not a fighter.
--Michael Jackson

Definition Word: Love
1. A deep and tender feeling of affection for or attachment or devotion to a person or persons. 2. An expression of one's love or affection. 3. A feeling of brotherhood and good will toward other people.

5:00 – 6:00
Book Study:

Michael Jackson

6:30 – 7:00pm
Writing Section:
In this section we will study and learn about Michael Jackson for thirty minutes, define the words we don't know or understand, and study product creation. During the completion of this book Michael Jackson died on June 25, 2009. We love you, and you will be truly missed, rest in peace Michael Jackson (MJ).

Michael Joseph Jackson (August 29, 1958- June 25, 2009) was an American musician and entertainer. The seventh child of the Jackson family, he debuted on the professional music scene at the age of eleven as a member of The Jackson 5. Jackson went on to begin a solo career in 1972, becoming a pop icon and named the "King of Pop". Five of his solo studio albums, "Off the Wall" (1979), "Thriller" (1982), "Bad" (1987), "Dangerous" (1991) and "HIStory" (1995), have become some of the world's best selling pop records.

Jackson became a dominant figure in popular music in the late 1970s as the first black entertainer to amass a strong crossover following on MTV. The popularity of his videos aired on MTV, such as "Beat It" and "Billie Jean", helped to put the relatively young channel "on the map", while videos such as "Black or White" and "Scream" made Jackson a staple on MTV into the 1990s. He transformed the music video into an art form and a promotional tool as well. Jackson popularized physically complicated dance techniques, such as the robot and the moonwalk, along with a distinctive musical sound and vocal style that have influenced numerous hip hop, pop, and R&B artists.

Jackson donated and raised several hundred million dollars for beneficial causes, through his Dangerous World Tour, charity singles and support of thirty-nine charities. Jackson was one of few artists to have been inducted into the Rock and Roll Hall of Fame twice. His awards include eight Guinness World Records—including one for "Thriller", as the worlds best selling album—thirteen Grammy Awards, thirteen number one singles in his solo career—more than any other artist in the Hot 100 era—and the sale of over 750 million units worldwide. Jackson's highly publicized personal life, coupled with his successful career, has made him a part of pop culture for almost four decades.

Product Creation: You Are Your Business

The one thing that business owners should realize is that you are your business. Everyday, I get up and work on my business. Whether I am at the store shopping, or walking my dog, I should have some representation of my business. I have become a walking billboard. Many don't agree, however I will wear my business name on me at all times. I will have it sown into my clothes, hats, shirts, etc. I can remember when these dot.com companies put their dot.com all over their cars. This is another good idea I have yet to use.

In order for your business to grow, people must know that you're there. They must be able to find you. I carry business cards everywhere I go and just pass them out through the course of the day as I meet different people. This is my life and my business and I have to take it seriously.

Kristen's Thoughts of the Day:
My sister Breon loves Michael Jackson. She doesn't care what the magazines have said about him. Michael Jackson has donated money to charities and he loved children. He is a really nice person.

Daddy's Thoughts of the Day:
In this section, my oldest daughter asked if we can add Michael Jackson as if she doesn't know everything about the man already. She loves him, so we did the book study on Michael Jackson. We talked about love, and how to remain in that state of mind when many may say bad things about you. I shared with them that they should never put their eyes or attention too much on the world and to stay focused on their goals. Keep your eyes on the prize, regardless of what people may say about you, never care about what others think. If they are not your friends or family, then what others say shouldn't even matter. Ignorance only responds to ignorance. Anytime you get scared, ask St. Michael the Archangel to take that fear out of your heart.

Day 32:
Hard Work Is a Must
Saturday May 10, 2008

Daily Meditation: Morning and Evening (6:00-6:10am) and (4:30-4:40pm)
Psalm 122:9
For the sake of the house of the Lord our God, I will seek your prosperity.

SUCCESSFUL SATURDAY

To have made it to Successful Saturday is truly a wonderful success. Throughout the week we have walked by faith, renewed our minds and spirit, and have trusted in the all powerful universe. We have maintained a wonderful character and we are thankful for whom we are and all that we have. To remain strong and in character throughout the week is truly defined as a success.

Children have never been very good at listening to their elders, but they have never failed to imitate them.
--James A. Baldwin

Definition Word: Meditation
1. Act of meditating; deep, continued thought
2. Solemn reflection on sacred matters as a devotional act
3. Oral or written material, as a sermon, based on meditation

5:00 – 6:00
Book Study:

James Baldwin
6:30 – 7:00pm
Writing Section: In this section we will study and learn about and James Baldwin for thirty minutes, define the words we don't know or understand, and study product creation.

James A. Baldwin served as the head football coach at Wake Forest from 1926 to 1927. His record at Wake Forest stands at 7-10-3. He also served as the head coach at Maine from 1919 to 1920, and at Duke University where he compiled a 6-1-2 record. He also served as the head coach of Duke's basketball program in 1922, compiling a 6-12 record.

He was the 15th head football coach for the Lehigh Mountain Hawks in Bethlehem, Pennsylvania and he held that position for three seasons, from 1922 until 1924. His overall coaching record at Lehigh was 13 wins, 8 losses, and 5 ties. This ranks him 13th at Lehigh in terms of total wins and eighth at Lehigh in terms of winning percentage

Product Creation: Hard Work Is a Must

If you're not willing to work hard in your business, then it will fail-plain and simple! At eighteen years of age I opened my business, King Industries, thinking that just because I had a business I was going to make some money. I wrote about it in my journal and my thinking back then was, let's just say, unprepared. I reopened my business last year and have been working hard to grow it. It's not easy, but this is what I love to do.

If you're not willing to put in the time to grow the business and go through the red tape, then you should hire someone to grow your business. But what new business owner has money for that? You have to put in the leg work until it gets big enough for you to hire employees to take on some of that responsibility.

Kristen's Thoughts of the Day:
He only had eight loses, how impressive! I wonder if he played on a football or basketball team when he was in college.

Daddy's Thoughts of the Day:
By example, I walk through life being the best role model I possibly can. And of course, I make my mistakes but I dust myself off and continue from where I stand. Life is not easy. No one told me that it would be easy, but they didn't tell me it would be this hard, either. My job as a parent is to provide the very best resources to equip them with opportunities. If there are no opportunities for them, they will have the skills to create their own. They will have the power to create whatever life they want and learn to pass that knowledge of their experience on to their kids. Seek! Seek! Seek! And you shall find life, peace, and abundance.

Day 33:
Common Mistakes of self Publishers
Sunday May 11, 2008

Daily Meditation: Morning and Evening (6:00-6:10am) and (4:30-4:40pm)
Psalm 72:7
In his days the righteous will flourish; prosperity will abound till the moon is no more.

SOULFUL SUNDAY

We should look to overflow our spirits with something good. A good word produces a good feeling. Today, we should remain in the place of peace, filling our soul with the joy and happiness from the word. Surround yourself with people of like faith and celebrate life. Remember to enjoy life on this day. Synagogue, temple, mosque, or church, whatever your faith, we should be humane to one another. Seek to fill yourself with an empowering word that will keep you motivated and inspired with the love you see all around us.

A man, as a general rule, owes very little to what he is born with - a man is what he makes of himself.
--Alexander Graham Bell

Definition Word: Productive
1: having the quality or power of producing especially in abundance 2: effective in bringing about

5:00 – 6:00
Book Study:

Alexander Graham Bell

6:30 – 7:00pm
Writing Section: In this section we will study and learn about and Alexander Graham Bell for thirty minutes, define the words we don't know or understand, and study product creation.

Alexander Graham Bell (March 3, 1847 – August 2, 1922) was an eminent scientist, inventor and innovator who are widely credited with the invention of the telephone. His father, grandfather and brother had all been associated with work on elocution and speech, and both his mother and wife were deaf, profoundly influencing Bell's life work. His research on hearing and speech further led him to experiment with hearing devices that eventually culminated in Bell being awarded the first U.S. patent for the invention of the telephone in 1876.

Many other inventions marked Bell's later life including groundbreaking work in hydrofoils and aeronautics. In 1888, Alexander Graham Bell became one of the founding members of the National Geographic Society. In reflection, Bell considered his most famous invention an intrusion on his real work as a scientist and refused to have a telephone in his study. Upon Bell's death, all telephones throughout the United States "stilled their ringing for a silent minute in tribute to the man whose yearning to communicate made them possible".

Product Creation: Common Mistakes of self Publishers

There are common mistakes self publishers make that can save you time and money if you avoid them. In this industry, to look professional you really have to dot your Is and cross your Ts. This will make the difference in having a professional appearance or not, which means sales. If self publishers would remember to avoid these seven mistakes, they would have a very promising and successful business.

1. Disregarding Your Business Plan
2. Disregarding Your ISBN Numbers
3. Disregarding Book Editing
4. Disregarding The Hiring of A Book Designer For The Layout Of Your Book
5. Disregarding The Bound Galley For Your Reviews
6. Disregarding To Get Your Book Proofread
7. Disregarding The Price For A Good Cover Design

Kristen's Thoughts of the Day:

He invented the telephone. I thought that was another person. Well he really did change people's lives.

Daddy's Thoughts of the Day:
We talk about the importance of being productive. I can't stop drilling this point into her psyche, if in fact I want what's best for her. I can't give her the world, but I can give her the words of God. Everyday, we should be actively working on our goals. The vision that I have for my family is impossible for me alone. I set our goals high and too far out of reach for just myself to accomplish. That way, when it is accomplished, I can truly say that there is a God!

Day 34:
Improve Your Credit
Monday May 12, 2008

Daily Meditation: Morning and Evening (6:00-6:10am) and (4:30-4:40pm)
Proverbs 29:18
"Where there is no vision the people perish..." KJV

MINDFULL MONDAY

As we return back to our regular schedule, keep in mind our experiences and the mistakes we have made. Create new opportunities and new approaches to situations we don't understand. Relax and think calmly on things that puzzle us. Ask for clarity and look for the answer. Seek always to make better choices than before. Be aware of what we think, do, and speak so that we can live a life that keeps us in the place of peace.

Faith and prayer are the vitamins of the soul; man cannot live in health without them.
--Mahalia Jackson

Definition Word: multi-talented
 4 a: more then one special, creative or artistic aptitude

5:00 – 6:00
Book Study:

Mahalia Jackson

6:30 – 7:00pm
Writing Section: In this section we will study and learn about and Mahalia Jackson for thirty minutes, define the words we don't know or understand, and study product creation.

Mahalia Jackson (October 26, 1911 – January 27, 1972) was an American Grammy Award-winning gospel singer, widely regarded as the best in the history of the genre. She is the first "Queen of Gospel Music". Mahalia Jackson became one of the most influential gospel singers in the world. She recorded about 30 albums (mostly for Columbia Records) during her career, and her 45 rpm records included a dozen "golds" and a million copies sold.

Product Creation: Improve Your Credit
Some people may wonder why credit is important. Well, credit tells a lot about a person. For one, it says that you pay off your debts. Why would an investor want to invest in a business when that person can't even pay off the debts they already have? It also shows a level of responsibility. When you are dealing with investors, you want to show that you are responsible and that they can depend on you.

Once you clear your credit and possess a well written business plan, doors will open for investment opportunities. Start building business credit with the products and services of Dun and Bradstreet. They have services that can help new businesses create business credit.

Kristen's Thoughts of the Day:
Mahalia Jackson became one of the most influential gospel singers in the world. Do you know how big that is? That's a big honor.

Daddy's Thoughts of the Day:
We used many examples throughout our book of studies of people being multi-talented. I wanted to show hard-working people doing many different things. Giving them ideas of what they might like to do with their life. We want to expose them to lots of different cultures, knowledge, and different ways of living by other societies. The world is at your finger tips. I am proud of both of my kids and I know that they will keep up the good work. So, I will plan for their future, writing it and creating it as we grow.

Day 35:
The Importance of a Journal
Tuesday May 13, 2008

Daily Meditation: Morning and Evening (6:00-6:10am) and (4:30-4:40pm)
Psalm 128:2
You will eat the fruit of your labor; Blessings and prosperity will be yours.

TRUSTFUL TUESDAY

Today choose faith over fear and make a conscious effort to be courageous and strong. As we trust in God, the choices we make, and the people in our lives believe that he will see us through to the next stage of our journey. We may not know what is going on at the present moment. Pray, meditate and just trust that God will take care of us. Have no doubts or fears about trusting in what God has planned for you regardless of whether you can see his plans or not, until his plans are revealed, just trust.

Thought is more important than art. To revere art and have no understanding of the process that forces it into existence, is finally not even to understand what art is.
--Amiri Baraka

Definition Word: Practice
2 a: to perform or work at repeatedly so as to become proficient

5:00 – 6:00
Book Study:

LeRoi Jones

6:30 – 7:00pm
Writing Section: In this section we will study and learn about and LeRoi Jones for thirty minutes, define the words we don't know or understand, and study product creation.

Baraka was born (October 7, 1934) as Everett LeRoi Jones in Newark, New Jersey, where he attended Barringer High School. His father, Coyette LeRoi Jones, worked as a postal supervisor and lift operator, and his mother, Anna Lois (née Russ), was a social worker. In 1952, he changed his name to LeRoi Jones. In 1967 he adopted the African name Imamu Ameer Baraka, which he later changed to Amiri Baraka.

Baraka studied philosophy and religious studies at Rutgers University, Columbia University and Howard University, without obtaining a degree. In 1954, he joined the US Air Force, reaching the rank of sergeant. After an anonymous letter to his commanding officer accusing him of being a communist led to the discovery of Soviet writings, Baraka was put on kitchen duty and given a dishonorable discharge for violation of his oath of duty.

The same year he moved to Greenwich Village, working initially in a warehouse for music records. His interest in jazz began in this period. At the same time, he came into contact with the incipient movement of Beat Poets powerfully influenced on his early poetry. In 1958, Jones founded Totem Press, which published such Beat icons as Jack Kerouac and Allen Ginsberg. The same year, he married Hettie Cohen and, with her, became joint editor of the Yugen literary magazine (until 1963).

In 1960 he went to Cuba, a visit that initiated his transformation into a politically active artist. In 1961, Preface to a Twenty Volume Suicide Note was published, followed in 1963 by Blues People: Negro Music in White America - to this day one of the most influential volumes of jazz criticism, especially in regard to the then beginning Free Jazz movement. His acclaimed controversial play "Dutchman" premiered in 1964 and received an Obie Award the same year. After the assassination of Malcolm X, Baraka broke free from the Beat Poets. He left his wife and their two children and moved to Harlem, considering himself at that time a black cultural nationalist. Later, Hettie Cohen, in her autobiography "How I Became Hettie Jones" (1996), claimed that Baraka had mistreated her during the time of their marriage.

Product Creation: The Importance of a Journal

Why should we keep a journal? A journal is a good way to evaluate yourself, to get a clear and precise understanding of events that may happen in our lives, yet we don't clearly understand why it continuously happens. A journal can tell of a mind set we may have been in a year ago, and we can use that to see how much we have grown over the course of the years, or not! It is designed so that you can see yourself and learn. Your writing and word organizational skills will improve, alone with sentence structure. A journal is also a good way to keep track of personal experiences that can be used at a later date, so if by chance you ever want to write a book, a journal is a good personal tool to help you further your skills and provide an accurate reflection of self.

Kristen's Thoughts of the Day:
When I heard the sentence that said Baraka studied philosophy and religious studies at Howard University, I thought to myself, where did I hear Howard University from? I figured out that my dad told me about Howard University. That's where he wants us to go to college.

Daddy's Thoughts of the Day:
Practice make perfect. Whatever your craft or talent, you have to practice it. God gave us all gifts and talents; however, we must practice to develop them. But what if you don't know what to practice, or what your talents are? You would have to find the answer to that famous question we all have asked ourselves at one point in our lives: "Who Am I?" You have to find your way and learn who you are. You do that through being exposed to many different activities. God has something for each of us to do. You have to explore everything and dedicate time to trying to develop it to see if you like it or not. You will know immediately if it matches who you are. But, you might set it down and never pick it up again. Or, you may not have enough money to put yourself in the position to practice your craft. What do you do then?

Daily Meditation: Morning and Evening (6:00-6:10am) and (4:30-4:40pm)
Proverbs 13:2
From the fruit of his lips a man enjoys good things, but the unfaithful have a craving for violence.

WONDERFUL WEDNESDAY

Throughout our day, we want to reflect on how blessed we are and how beautiful life is. We want to do our best to honor ourselves and our spirit. We want to remain humble throughout the day, never forgetting that God is not mocked. We want to remember to work hard at accomplishing our goals and increasing our talents and skills, stay focused on the task at hand so that we may excel in all that we do. Put forth effort at being the best person we can be, knowing that we are whole, together, generous, balanced, and well-rounded. We will not be afraid to let our light shine through and make a difference in the lives of others. Regardless of what the day may bring, we will remain in the position of Godliness.

It takes courage to grow up and become who you really are.
--E. E. Cummings

To be nobody but yourself in a world which is doing its best, night and day, to make you everybody else means to fight the hardest battle which any human being can fight; and never stop fighting.
--E. E. Cummings

Definition Word: Will
1. The power to make your own choices and decisions 2.Being able to control your own actions.

5:00 – 6:00
Book Study:
                                E.E. Cummings

6:30 – 7:00pm
Writing Section: In this section we will study and learn about and E. E. Cummings for thirty minutes, define the words we don't know or understand, and study product creation.

Edward Estlin Cummings (October 14, 1894 – September 3, 1962), popularly known as E. E. Cummings, was an American poet, painter, essayist, author, and playwright. His body of work encompasses more than 900 poems, several plays and essays, numerous drawings, sketches, and paintings, as well as two novels. He is remembered as a preeminent voice of 20th century poetry, as well as one of the most popular.

As we continue to learn about different people, we will also study and talk about ways to grow and maintain our businesses. Bookkeeping is the subject and is very well needed in all business success. We read from *Black Enterprise's Guide to Starting Your Own Business* Chapter 12.

We read for an hour and recorded it in our book as a reference to come back to and study at a later date. This is like our own text book we are writing for ourselves. The purpose of our book is to come back to study it when we need it. She will not learn how to run and manage a business in forty days; however, she can make a reference as to where she can find the information she needs.

Product Creation: Establish a Strong Network
My grandmother had this saying, "Lie down with dogs you will come up with fleas". And my mother would tell me, "Birds of a feather flock together". These sayings hold true in all areas of life. One of the most important things you will have to do is surround yourself with other people who are trying to do the same things as you. Build a strong network. Your network should have key people in it that will take your business to another level.

Create a list of investors and incorporate them into your network. Your network should be strong and willing to work just as hard as you for the common goal of achieving wealth. With that understood, all should work to accomplish the tasks at hand to bring your business to the level of growth you want it to be. Look around you and the friends you see represent the person you will become.

Kristen's Thoughts of the Day:
I enjoyed learning about E.E.Cummings because he has such an interesting life. I liked the part when they said that his body of work amounts to more than 900 poems, several plays and essays, many drawings, sketches, and paintings, and two novels. When I heard that, I was thinking, that's impressive. He has written a lot.

Daddy's Thoughts of the Day:
I can see you now in the future and, through your dedication and hard-work you have grown to become a woman of powerful words. Practice makes perfect and keep up the fight, learn, grow, teach, heal....Do your best to be the best in whatever God has for you to do.

Day 37:
Establish Many Legs of Income
Thursday May 15, 2008

Daily Meditation: Morning and Evening (6:00-6:10am) and (4:30-4:40pm)
Proverbs 21:21
He who pursues righteousness and love finds life, prosperity and honor.

THANKFUL THURSDAY

Today we want to give thanks remembering all the things we should be thankful for. We should choose to be thankful for our experiences good or bad, friends, family, and most importantly our health. We should be thankful for who we are now and what we are to become. Let your words of thanksgiving be received through your prayers, your spirit, your actions and your songs. Be still in your spirit and anxious for nothing but thankful for all.

If the First Amendment means anything, it means that a state has no business telling a man, sitting alone in his house, what books he may read or what films he may watch.
--Thurgood Marshall

Definition Word: Revolutionary
1. Bringing about or constituting a great or radical change

5:00 – 6:00
Book Study:
Thurgood Marshall

6:30 – 7:00pm
Writing Section: In this section we will study and learn about and Thurgood Marshall for thirty minutes, define the words we don't know or understand, and study product creation.

Thurgood Marshall (July 2, 1908 – January 24, 1993) was an American jurist and the first African American to serve on the Supreme Court of the United States. Before becoming a judge, he was a lawyer who was best remembered for his high success rate in arguing before the Supreme Court and for the victory in Brown v. Board of Education.

Marshall was born in Baltimore, Maryland on July 2, 1908. His original name was Thoroughgood but he shortened it to Thurgood in second grade. His father, William Marshall, instilled in him an appreciation for the Constitution of the United States and the rule of law. Additionally, as a child, he was punished for his school misbehavior by being forced to read the Constitution, which he later said piqued his interest in the document. Marshall was a descendant of slaves.

Marshall was married twice; to Vivian "Buster" Burey from 1929 until her death in February 1955 and to Cecilia Suyat from December 1955 until his own death in 1993. He had two sons from his second marriage; Thurgood Marshall, Jr., who is a former top aide to President Bill Clinton, and John W. Marshall, who is a former United States Marshals Service Director and since 2002 has served as Virginia Secretary of Public Safety under Governors Mark Warner and Tim Kaine.

Product Creation: Establish Many Legs of Income

What I have learned through my journey of e-commerce is that the experts have many different ways of making money. They don't just stop at one product, which may be a book, but they may have rental property, videos, and audio products as well. They realize that in order to become wealthy you must have other avenues of making money and not just rely on one income stream to create wealth.

For instance, we at King Industries Community Development Center also have a real estate company with one house, as of now. However, with the production of this book, we now have enough money to reinvest more money into our real estate company, allowing us to continue to grow our businesses. We have a team of people that are dedicated to growing the business and creating wealth for themselves.

We have three more books in production right now and other businesses being created and established. These will create further income streams, which we will reinvest to create more wealth for the businesses, and its occupants as a whole. Exploring several ways of creating income is vital to creating wealth. That is the difference between creating a business as a job and creating a business to create wealth. I didn't create these businesses to just work another job; I created these businesses so that I can hire someone to do the job for me. I created these businesses to create jobs for others. Therefore, you have to create several ways of making money in order to become wealthy and provide jobs in the community at the same time.

Kristen's Thoughts of the Day:
When I heard that he was the first African American to serve on the Supreme Court of the United States, I was thinking, that's cool because I want to be a judge too.

Daddy's Thoughts of the Day:
I want her to think about the future and where she will be. At an early age, I have my children thinking about their lives and how they can make them better. What can be done to change your present situation? If there was one thing you could change right now, what would it be? You're blessed and I want you to know just how blessed you are. I want you to understand this.

Day 38:
Duplicate the Process
Friday May 16, 2008

Daily Meditation: Morning and Evening (6:00-6:10am) and (4:30-4:40pm)
Ecclesiastes 6:6
Even if he lives a thousand years twice over but fails to enjoy his prosperity. Do not all go to the same place?

FAITHFUL FRIDAY

Its important that we awaken to all that we are meant to be through our journey in life. Our faithfulness to ourselves will allow us to be patient in life as we become more of who we are meant to be. We should be faithful in longsuffering, bearing of pain, and dealing with trials without complaint. We should be faithful in showing self-control with others, as well as ourselves. Our faith will cause us to fight against any adversity, cause us to be focused, and fearless. Have faith throughout this day.

If there's a book you really want to read, but it hasn't been written yet, then you must write it.
--Toni Morrison

Definition Word: longsuffering
We will learn longsuffering and the ability to "never give up". We must trust God unconditionally. This is the means by which Jesus accomplished all that God intended for Him to do. It's the same with us.

5:00 – 6:00
Book Study:

Toni Morrison

6:30 – 7:00pm
Writing Section: In this section we will study and learn about and Toni Morrison for thirty minutes, define the words we don't know or understand, and study product creation.

Toni Morrison (born Chloe Anthony Wofford on February 18, 1931), is a Nobel Prize-winning American author, editor, and professor. Her novels are known for their epic themes, vivid dialogue, and richly detailed black characters; among the best known are her novels *The Bluest Eye*, *Song of Solomon*, and *Beloved*, which won the Pulitzer Prize for Fiction in 1988. In 2001, she was named one of the "30 Most Powerful Women in America" by Ladies' Home Journal.

Product Creation: Duplicate the Process

If you notice, the entire process of product creation and being successful in the ecommerce industry is duplication. Every internet millionaire has a product, a way to deliver that product, and a good marketing strategy, which is a key factor in this industry. I have known people to make $90,000 working one day, due to their marketing strategy.

There are two primary means of making money online: through direct sales of products and through affiliate programs. Your marketing strategy should be precise and enthusiastic. You should be excited about making money, so let your excitement shine through to your customers. Post your message on ezines, google, youtube, etc. Get out there and make it happen! With a good product and a good message to attract your audience, you could make a lot of money. Make sure your website is set up to handle your orders.

Learn different marketing strategies and attend seminars and educational groups to help you get where you need to go. A good thing to establish is a network of people doing the same thing as you. And find a coach! With a mentor you can't go wrong. There are people, who have done what you're trying to do now; who have been in your shoes. Take their advice and use it. Duplicate their process; if it worked for them, why not you?

Kristen's Thoughts of the Day:
From the stories I've heard about her books, it's making me want to read them. They say that she puts epic themes, vivid dialogue, and richly detailed black characters in her books.

Daddy's Thoughts of the Day:
I want Kristen to learn that sometimes, one must work hard on one job to get to the next step. Use things as stepping stones and never give up on climbing to the next level. Longsuffering is one of God's ways of testing your worthiness. God is

testing your guts, strength, and power. God wants to know if you are really ready to handle the new set of responsibilities he has for you. Nothing comes easy; if it does, give it back because you don't want it. You want to work hard for what you get so that you can appreciate it to the fullest.

In the pursuit of training my kids about money and business, I show them the process of starting a non-profit organization and how a non-profit organization works. I tell them the name of our organization, King Industries Community Development Center, and how it will be used. To revitalize a community that needs economic development. King will give seminars and have programs in the areas of business and real-estate. We will also explore more of holistic healing of the mind and body and creating more spiritual programs to help with confidence and science programs that will bring awareness of the newest of technologies.

And again, I want them to know that these are the areas that they must learn and grow in before they can take over any of these businesses created for them to operate for the advancement of their lives. I teach them that they must do their part in helping to make this world a better place to live, for themselves, their kids, as well as humanity. We all are called but very few answer.

Perfection and its principles

"be ye, therefore, perfect, even as your Father, which is in heaven, is perfect."
–Mathew 5:48

Perfect or being perfect is to have your affirmations. Your positive thoughts will align with God (the universe). We put time and energy into sharpening ourselves and trust unconditionally that our goals and plans will come to pass. What happens when we make ourselves perfect? When we meditate and vibrate those thoughts of affirmation we become as perfect as we can become here on earth, in our bodies.

Day 39:
Conquer Your Fear to Acquire Wealth
Saturday May 17, 2008

Daily Meditation: Morning and Evening (6:00-6:10am) and (4:30-4:40pm)
Proverbs 3:1-2
My son, do not forget my teaching,
     but keep my commands in your heart,
 2 for they will prolong your life many years
     and bring you prosperity.

SUCCESSFUL SATURDAY

To have made it to Successful Saturday is truly a wonderful success. Throughout the week we have walked by faith, renewed our minds and spirit, and have trusted in the all powerful universe. We have maintained a wonderful character and we are thankful for whom we are and all that we have. To remain strong and in character throughout the week is truly defined as a success.

Definition Word: Persistence
How badly do you want your goal(s) and what determination you'll use to get there?

5:00 – 6:00
Book Study:
Starting a Publishing Company

6:30 – 7:00pm
Writing Section: In this section we will study and learn about and Starting a Publishing Company for thirty minutes, define the words we don't know or understand, and study product creation.

As you know, Kristen, your goal was to start a business. So, I'd like you to go to this website and tell me about the Secretary of States. I asked her to tell me what it meant and she looked it up:

The Secretary of State also is responsible for registering business entities (corporations, etc.) and granting them the authority to do business within the state, registering secured transactions, and granting access to public documents.

I thanked her for becoming a great eleven-year-old secretary. Then I told her this story about this bird in Africa, the Secretary bird.

Secretary bird, common name for a long-legged African bird, Sagittarius serpentarius, related to the hawk and about 4 ft (122 cm) tall. Its crest of black feathers suggested the quill pens behind the ear of a 19th-century male secretary. The bird hunts on foot, zigzagging toward its prey and flapping its wings, and is valued as a destroyer of snakes and other reptiles. Secretary birds are classified in the phylum Chordata, subphylum Vertebrata, and class Aves, and order Falconiformes, family Sagittariidae.

I then showed her the form that she needed to fill out in order to start a Limited Liability Companies (LLC). You would get the Articles of Organization (LLC-1) when you get this form (LLC-1) FOLLOW INSTRUCTIONS FOR COMPLETING THE ARTICLES OF ORGANIZATION (FORM LLC-1). Send $70.00 and that's it.

I want to show her the start of a legacy, that being the age she is and living during the dawn of a black president, good times will ensuc. I want her to grow up with her businesses being a part of her, or second nature. While working in her businesses producing money, we share and give part of it back to God. Through the non-profit organization, we reform communities by creating self sufficient homes, sustainable by solar energy, and other energy products, one home at a time. Each business King starts gives 20% back to King for the refunding of its endeavors for continued community growth.

Businesses King Industries Community Development Center has started:

❖ M&J Property Consultants, LLC
❖ Jonestown Publishing, LLC
❖ Malone's Nursing Consultants, LLC.
❖ Mastiff Express, LLC.
❖ Kribre Beauty Supplies, LLC

We try to employ our family members with jobs so that they will have added income, hoping that through love and business, we can impact this community in a more positive way. This is our way of giving back to the community. Through All Good Works, we help our people start and manage their own businesses within their own communities, bringing the economy of that area up and putting $500 billion of black consumer monies back into the communities of which we live. I want to raise my kids with the understanding of community reform. I also want them to gain the knowledge of documenting experiences, such as those in the Rites of Passage Program, in books.

1. California Secretary of State:

California Secretary of State
1500 11th Street
Sacramento, California 95814
(916) 653-6814
http://www.sos.ca.gov/business/

To start any business, you will have to file with the Secretary of state in which you reside. We live in California and we wanted our business to be California based, so we filed through the California Secretary of State. Any business you would start, you would have to go through the Secretary of State of that state.

2. Limited Liability Companies
I asked Kristen to go here and start thinking of a name and what she would do. The Rites of Passage Program Coordinator is her aunt, Tiffany R. Jones. Through the program, we went through the whole process with Kristen so that she could have a product to sell by the end of her forty days. By selling her Rites of Passage experience, she will start to see and live a life with entrepreneurial experience. That's the type of experiences I want in our lives and we hope that you get the same results. Be well and prosperous.

Once on the site, go to Business Programs, business entities. Limited Liability Companies

We looked at the LLC's for her to start her own Publishing Co., Jonestown Publishing, LLC. She went online herself and found the form and we filled them out. I showed her the

Business Programs Division
FORMS, SAMPLES & FEES
(916) 657-5448

Articles of Organization (LLC-1) (Domestic LLC)
From the website, you will find your business entities and Limited Liability Companies. Fill out these forms and return them with $70.00. Kristen got the forms, we went over them together and she did the good job of mailing them off. I gave her the money and it was a fun and good experience.

3. DBA County Clerk's office: A Fictitious Business Name is $30.00
You would get a DBA, Doing Business As, then whatever you want to name your business. It's an easy process, but an important one. You have to be careful of the name because it will represent you and your business identity. This identifies you and your product; it sets you apart from the competition. Be careful how you choose.

4. A Federal Tax ID Number (EIN). Some banks require only your EIN to open a business bank account. Some require both your EIN and your DBA. You need an EIN for your business taxes. If you plan on having more than one employee, you would use this number for tax purposes. To open your business bank account, you would need your EIN. To obtain a business line of credit, and if you're forming an LLC, Corporation, or a Partnership, you will need EIN.

You can easily obtain your EIN by going to: http://www.irs.gov/businesses/, you can call for your EIN number over the phone for free, or you can mail your form in to the IRS.

5. This book is the instructions to my family as well as me. We honor them and believe in them as being filled with the word of God. We published it so that it would be a part of our family history. If I wanted to write a book with my daughter, this is what I would want it to say. We free ourselves through reading, music, knowledge and writing.

6. To further educate yourself about the advantages and disadvantages of your business you should seek professional help. If you need funding and you have never done it before, consult your professionals.

132

Product Creation: Conquer Your Fear and Acquire Wealth

Being afraid to create a product is losing out on opportunity and money. I came to realize that being afraid kept me from living my dreams. Now, I have a beautiful life and am very happy working for myself. When I did the calculations on paper, I had a target of 2500 sales to reach my goal of $9375. I started thinking and looking at my emails and all of my family and friends and their friends. I looked at all the social websites like Myspace, twitter, facebook and Youtube. I realized that 2500 sales are very easy to achieve and it can, and will, be done on a continuous basis.

A little marketing tip: Join every social site, business network, and group to maximize your exposure. If its traffic you want then you must have your hands into everything. Get heavily involved in your marketing strategy and learn as much as you can about e-commerce.

I remember before becoming a merchant seaman, I was living in Tujunga, Ca. outside of Glendale, and had a job working security while going to school. It seemed like nothing was going right for me and time was standing still. Living paycheck to paycheck, I didn't have enough money to do anything. After four years of being in the same position, I decided to make a change. I asked my partner to go back home with the kids to New Orleans, La. while I made some moves.

A month after my family left, I was out on the street homeless. I wrecked my Jeep Grand Cherokee, lost my job and had no where to stay. I soon got a job while still living out of my truck. That one job helped me apply for the merchant marines and, after nine months of homelessness, I was out on the ship. I called my family back to California and I started shipping as much as possible. After three years of shipping, I now have three businesses, a book published, and two rental properties.

Sometimes, the bad things that happen in your life are a blessing in disguise. And when it comes to being afraid, I don't have time or the patience to be afraid. I'm more afraid of being homeless than afraid of being rejected, because someone doesn't like my products or services. Now, I follow my heart and my gut. If I have an idea, I pursue it with everything I have and to me, there is no such thing as failure! I'm going to make it happen. You'd better believe that. I'm not going back on the street for anyone!

Kristen's Thoughts of the Day:
This all seems so interesting and it's a good idea too.

Daddy's Thoughts of the Day:
Kristen I want you to learn to complete your goal given by your Aunt Tiffany, the coordinator of our business program. I am proud of her for following the direction and for being such a, "good sport" through the frothy days of spiritual growth and mind expansion. You did your best, now watch, and see what measure of your work will come back to you. My kids must know that it will become hard for them in life, and in business, and they will need persistence to come out on top. The strength to continue pressing forward without fainting is persistence. Be optimistic and find a way when it seems like there is no way at all. Just remember that, I will always be there for you!

I want to talk about the Principle of prayer.

Daily we must do whatever it is we do to communicate with God. I use meditation and send out my thoughts, imaginations, and feelings, through the universe. Many people have their own way of doing this, and whatever works best for you is fine. This should be a prayer that puts you in favor, alignment, or in a harmonious rhythm with us and the universe at one time, simultaneously.

"Blessed is the person who walketh not in the counsel of the ungodly, nor standeth in the way of sinners, nor sitteth in the seat of the scornful. But their delight is in the law of the Lord; and in this law do they meditate day and night."-Psalms 1:1-2

We, at King Industries, teach our members the importance of guilt by association. That goes for people that respond to negative thoughts, feeling, emotions, and activities in a negative way. These kinds of thoughts will not bring us what we want in our lives. So we must stay away from these kinds of people. We are to accomplish our goals and move forward with our life, without all the negativity. Through positive thinking good fortune comes. Everyday focus your thoughts and thinking in truth.

I want to also record the principle of forgiveness

"For if you forgive men when they sin against you, your heavenly Father will also forgive you. But if you do not forgive men their sins, your Father will not forgive your sins." –Mathew 6:14-15

Whatever has hurt you or hindered you from moving forward in your life, you must let it go in order to free yourself so that you can become successful in your life. Holding on to the past is like a ball and chain tied to your leg and someone dropping you in the ocean. You can't move forward in your life carrying all that weight. Let it go, in order to release yourself from negative emotions, guilt, insecurity, and self-sabotage.

Daily Meditation: Morning and Evening (6:00-6:10am) and (4:30-4:40pm)
Proverbs 3:3
"Let love and faithfulness never leave you; bind them around your neck,
write them on the tablet of your heart".

SOULFUL SUNDAY

We should look to overflow our spirits with something good. A good word produces a good feeling. Today, we should remain in the place of peace, filling our soul with the joy and happiness from the word. Surround yourself with people of like faith and celebrate life. Remember to enjoy life on this day. Synagogue, temple, mosque, or church, whatever your faith, we should be humane to one another. Seek to fill yourself with an empowering word that will keep you motivated and inspired with the love you see all around us.

Change will not come if we wait for some other person or some other time. We are the ones we've been waiting for. We are the change that we seek.
--Barack Obama

Definition Word: Outstanding
1: standing out; projecting 2 a: unpaid b: continuing to exist: unresolved 3 a: standing out from a group: conspicuous b: marked by eminence and distinction

5:00 – 6:00
Book Study:

Barack Obama

6:30 – 7:00pm
Writing Section: In this section we will study and learn about and Barack Obama for thirty minutes, define the words we don't know or understand, and study product creation.

Barack Hussein Obama, Jr. (born August 4, 1961) is the junior United States Senator from Illinois and the presumptive nominee of the Democratic Party in the 2008 presidential election. He is the first African American to be the presumptive presidential nominee of any major American political party.

A graduate of Columbia University and Harvard Law School, Obama worked as a community organizer, taught constitutional law, and also worked as a political activist and lawyer before serving in the Illinois Senate from 1997 to 2004. Following an unsuccessful bid for a seat in the U.S. House of Representatives in 2000, he announced his campaign for the U.S. Senate in January 2003. After winning a landslide primary victory in March 2004, Obama delivered the keynote address at the Democratic National Convention in July 2004. He was elected to the U.S. Senate in November 2004 with 70% of the vote.

As a member of the Democratic minority in the 109th Congress, he cosponsored legislation to control conventional weapons and to promote greater public accountability in the use of federal funds. He also made official trips to Eastern Europe, the Middle East, and Africa. In the current 110th Congress, he has sponsored legislation regarding lobbying and electoral fraud; climate change, nuclear terrorism, and care for returned U.S. military personnel. Since announcing his presidential campaign in February 2007, Obama has emphasized ending the war in Iraq, increasing energy independence, decreasing the influence of lobbyists, and providing universal health care as top national priorities.

Product Creation: Product Complete

For thirty minutes a day for forty days, we have researched product creation and have written our notes on the subject. You should now have enough material to produce your own products to sell online. Make sure to copyright your work and hit the web. Get excited, enthusiastic, and have fun making money with your new products. As you dive into this wonderful world of internet marketing, you should have enough information to make a handsome return on the work that you have done. Have fun with it and Good Luck!

Kristen's Thoughts of the Day:
I think he is a good man and he would be perfect for president. I want him to win because he's convincing and if he wins, he would be the first black president.

Daddy's Thoughts of the Day:
I think history is being made; Barack Obama, a black man, is running for president of the United States. Yes, a lot has changed and much more will change, but it's up to each individual to step up and do their part in the whole humanitarian scheme of things. We need to get out there and vote to make sure that we get the right man into office. I think Barack Obama, if he became president, will make a gallant effort to change the present state of recession the United States currently faces. I know if he becomes president, he will work hard to make America and the world a better place.

That is why we used examples of all these people that were/are in the real world, to show what the true meaning of work is. Being happy doing something you love all day is happiness and real! Be in God; for me, there is no other way to go. Now that I have learned how to create my own money and to provide for my family, I will never work a nine-to-five ever again. I am my own BOSS! My job as a Merchant Marine is over! I will never again have to leave my family to work on a ship four to eight months at a time.

So, as you know, everything in life must start with you. As we read and gain knowledge, you will find that we are all afforded the same rights and must take advantage of the right to freedom of speech. It's a matter of if you want it or not.

I want my family to learn the power of a pen. I want them to be a part of history, by writing their own history. I want them to know how to create their history at will with their pen! That is what the book study and lessons were all about.

Everything in life starts with you.
1. You must take action (Spread the word and vote.)
2. You must pray.
3. You must exercise discipline.
4. You must sharpen your talents or craft.

Become the master of self and all prosperity you have been blessed with.

Spread the Good News:
Barack asked us this, 'Please cover me with your prayers...cover me, Michelle, and my family with your prayers'. Then he stretched out his arms, before the group 'A blanket of prayer to cover us all that is what I am asking of you. Pray for me'.
- A Prayer for Barack -

'Father, in the Name of Jesus, we lift up your son Barack Obama on our prayers and praises. We thank you for a time such as this and for sending a man such as Barack to fulfill your work in our land. We blanket Barack, Michelle, and his family in our prayers, our love, our warm thoughts, our positive energy, and our spiritual forces. We ask that you cover him and his family with your precious blood. We stand resolute in prayer and in absolute power against any and all negative forces or spirits of darkness, ignorance, and hatred that would seek to destroy your handiwork. O Lord, Barack is Your Handiwork. And we praise, worship, and honor you for the great things you are doing and will do through his hands. In Jesus' Name ... **Amen**.'

Conclusion

In conclusion, we as parents want the best for our kids. So we diligently create and build for their future. We must not take away their possibilities and we must work hard to create them. I have heard people say many times, "Get your head out of the clouds". I feel that phrase destroys a child's beliefs about what he or she can or cannot do. If a child believes something is unattainable, most of the time they will not have what they think they can't have. A child can grow up to be anything they want to be, do anything they want to do. That is, according to their belief: only if they believe it, can they do all things. Like Philippians 4:13 says, "I can do all things through Christ Jesus which strengthens me".

We, at King Industries Community Development Center, are dedicated to preserving that which is possible. So, what is possible? Is writing a book with your eleven year old daughter possible? My answer was yes! Once this book is completed we are off to write our second book as another product for King Industries. We create products as books so the organization can sell the books as a product. Selling the products we create generate capital for future activities of King Industries Community Development Center.

Our second book from King Industries is a book about our family businesses. It is in the same format but the information is different. We are telling of the success of one of the companies King Industries has started, a Real Estate Investing Company called M&J Property Consultants. We started this company in February of 2009. We will learn about business management and our knowledge on money thus far. What we will share is how to manage a business and how to manage money.

I want to give my kids within our organization the knowledge of money at an early age. I want them to grow with this knowledge well into their teens and carry it with them through life, knowing how to manage money and businesses. The possibility for success is greater when we equip our kids with the tools needed for tomorrow's economy. We look towards the future and realize they will need developed skills in the sciences, math, and finances: That is why King Industries was created, to develop programs that would teach the kids of today science, math, and business for tomorrow. We teach them to plan today for their future.

Everything they learn and write down I want them to save as if it was treasure. I have them put everything in a book so they can read what they have learned throughout the years, preserving it with an ISBN, like a printed journal. They can have it for years and be able to look back and reread what they wrote and learned at that age. Now, they can see their growth and what areas they may need to improve on.

Many people have come to me and shared their money-making secrets. Their ideas, philosophies, and information that could change the lives of anyone that would but use the information given. As you start to collect information, it becomes apart of your library so that you have the power now to do with it as you choose. I grant first my family and friends with love, money, success, happiness, and most importantly good health.

I had a guy ask me, "How can you grant them all these things with just the information you have?" What he fails to understand is we all have the power within us right now to be extremely successful if only we believe. Information is very valuable if you know how and when to use it. You have a wealth of knowledge, so what are you going to do with it, and how will you use it?

Le Garrius Jones

LeGarrius T. Jones, CEO